Latin Made Simple Through Stories

EASY LATIN

CONTENTS

INTRODUCTION

This book was created in conjunction with the Easy Latin Youtube channel found here (where you can find audio lessons):

https://www.youtube.com/channel/UC3ArArRlFe-aAM-I4SbfvsQ

The most effective way to learn a language is in context, because not only is it easier to learn new words this way, but you will also acquire grammar organically. And it's much more fun and interesting to learn this way than to memorize grammar tables. In these book, we will be learning directly from simple sentences in Latin and you may be surprised how easily and quickly you will acquire this beautiful language. Let's go!

LESSON 1

Salvēte omnēs!   Hi everybody!

We'll start with this sentence, which is in present tense. Can you guess what it means?

Poeta scribit.   [poh-AY-tuh   SCREE-bit]

Poeta should be obvious and if you recall words like "scribe, scribble, script," you can probably figure out that "scribit" means write. But wait, there are only two words. Is this sentence complete? Yes, actually, in Latin there are no words corresponding to "a" or "the." This has to be pulled from context, so Poeta scribit can mean "the poet writes" or "a poet writes" depending on the sentence that came before it.

Discipula studet.   [dis-KIP-uh-luh STUD-et]

Looking at the second word, can you guess the first? Who is it that studies? A disciplined disciple is a...student, right? That's right, this means "The student studies". Or "A student studies". Notice that the "c" in Discipula is a hard sound like a k. This is always the case for classical Latin, C's never make a "sss" sound.   Okay, now how would we say, The student writes? Can you remember?

Discipula scribit.

And The poet studies?

Poeta studet.
Now let's change it up a little.

Ego studeo.   [EGG-oh   STUD-eh-oh]

Do you see how we changed from studet to studeo? This is like the change from studies to study, so we know that the subject of this sentence is somehow different. Now, someone with a big ego is always thinking about themselves, so it's easy to remember that Ego means I. This sentence means "I study".

Now, for "I write" we won't be able to guess the form, following the pattern above, because it's:

Ego scribo.   [EGG-oh   SCREE-boh]

So we have, so far:

Poeta scribit.   Poeta studet.

Discipula scribit.   Discipula studet.

Ego scribo.   Ego studeo.

Now I'm going to add lines over some of the vowels, but don't worry, these will actually make pronunciation easier. These signify that the vowel is long, just like in elementary school. You can note the difference in the word scrībit, where there is one long and one short vowel.

Poēta scrībit.   Poēta studet.

Discipula scrībit.   Discipula studet.

Ego scrībō.   Ego studeō.

Let's add another verb:

Discipula legit.   [dis-KIP-uh-luh   LEG-it]

When something is legible, we are able to...read it. But notice that, just like the "c" in Discipula, the "g" in Latin is always a hard sound. Now look at the conjugation for scrībit and studet. Can you guess how to say, "I read"?

8

Ego legō.   [EGG-oh LEG-oh]   (leggo my eggo ;)
The word "you" in Latin is tū with a long vowel.   You = tū - pretty easy to remember, huh? And for our two verbs we have:

    tū scrībis   [two   SCREE-bis]
    tū studēs   [two   STUD-ays]
    tū legis   [two   LEG-is]

Are you starting to see a pattern?

    Ego   -ō
    Tū   -s
    (It) -t

Verbs conjugated with Ego always end with a long ō. When the subject is Tū, the verb always ends with s. And for third person singular, the verb ends in t. The only difficult part is that the vowel sometimes changes before these endings, but there are only a few conjugation patterns, so it's not that bad. Let's add another verb.

    Discipula dormit   [dis-KIP-uh-luh DOR-mit]

The Tū form is a little different from what we've seen. It has a long ī vowel:

    Tū dormīs   [two   DOR-mees]

Now, what do you think this sentence means:

    Agricola dormit.   [uh-GRIH-cola DOR-mit]

Look at the first four letters. This is a person that has something to do with AGRICulture - i.e. a farmer.

And what does this mean:

    Agricola labōrat.   [uh-GRIH-cola luh-BOH-ruht]

Chop off the "at" and we have labor, or work. And "I work" would be?

For the Tū form we have a change again, but you might be able to guess it from labōrat. You work is:

    Tū labōrās.   [two   luh-BOH-rahs]

9

Now we have seen all the different verb patterns. Let's put them all together.

Ego	labōr_-ō	scrīb_-ō	stude-ō	dormi-ō
Tū	labōrā-s	scrībi-s	studē-s	dormī-s
(It)	labōra-t	scrībi-t	stude-t	dormi-t

Note the differences and similarities in the patterns:

1.   All verbs end in either ō, s, or t,
2.   The vowel before ō is dropped half of the time.
3.   The vowel before the s in the Tū form is almost always long, just like the ū in Tū is long.

What we think of as dictionary for a verb (e.g. "to work") is known as the infinitive form. For the verbs we've learned so far, this looks like:

labōrāre   scrībere   studēre   dormīre

As you can see, the vowel before "re" in scrībere [SCREE-beh-reh] is short, just like the Tū form for this verb. But again, don't try to memorize these rules, because that's no fun, and you will naturally learn them as we work through more verbs, like this one:

Discipula discit.   [dis-KIP-uh-luh   DISK-it]

We already learned Discipula studet, so can you think of something else students do? It's a little hard to guess, so I'll just give away that this means learns.

Discipula discit. = The student learns.

Look at this next sentence. What do you think "et" means?

Discipula legit et discit.   [LEG-it et DISK-it]

This word is used in the famous line from Shakespeare's play Julius Caesar, when he says, "Et tū, Brute?" And you Brutus? He says this after he sees that his friend Brutus is one of his assassins and the phrase is often alluded to in literature when there is an unexpected betrayal by a friend. So "et" means "and".

From the sentence Ego discō, can you figure out how to say "You study and learn?"

Tū studēs et discis.   [STUD-ays et DISK-is]

Did you remember the short "i" sound? Now try to say, "You work and write and study and sleep".

Tū labōrās et scrībis et studēs et dormīs.

The next word doesn't have as easy of an association with an English word. But thinking of magistrate or maestro might help. A Magistra is a teacher. And what does a teacher do?

Magistra docet.   [muh-GIH-struh   DOCK-et]

A teacher teaches.   This verb has ties to indoctrinate and doctrine. Also someone who is docile is teachable. And it's easy to remember if you know what a docent is. The infinitive is docēre, so how do we say I teach and you teach in Latin?

Ego doceō et tū docēs.   [DOCK-eh-oh] [DOCK-ays]

We're now ready to tackle our first proverb in Latin. That's kind of amazing, isn't it?

Quī docet, discit.   [kwee DOCK-et   DISK-it]

Look at the first word. The WH wh sound in English is a QU sound in Latin, so if you see a short word starting with Qu, it most likely means Who what where when or why. Since we know what docet and discit mean, can you guess the meaning of this sentence? It's actually not a question.

It means literally, "Who teaches, learns". Or more elegantly phrased: "He who teaches, learns".

Don't worry if you don't remember everything from this lesson, we will be repeating everything along the way.

But before we end this lesson, one final note: Did you notice that all the nouns in this lesson end in "a"? We'll see why I chose them in the next lesson.

GRAMMAR INTERLUDE

Before we move on to the next lesson, we need to make a brief foray into grammar. But don't worry, this will be painless.

Sometimes in order to learn a foreign language, we have to learn a little more about our native language first, since we use many aspects of grammar intuitively and since some languages use certain aspects of grammar in different ways than other languages.

In English, word order can change the meaning of a sentence. For example, one of the following sentences is more surprising than the other:

Dog bites man.   Man bites dog.

This is because in English, the first noun is the subject – the doer of the verb.

And the noun following the verb is the object – what the verb acts on.

In this way, English is classified as an SVO language.
Subject - verb - object.

But Latin does not have fixed word order, the words have to change form in order for us to tell which word is which. This might seem strange at first, but we also do this for some words in English. Notice, we don't say:

I give he the book.

We change he to him because it is the recipient – which is also called the indirect object. HE is only used as the subject. So we have seen that nouns can have three different kinds of jobs in the sentence so far. I, the subject, him, the recipient, and the book, the object, or what the verb acts on.

12

In English, word order usually tells us everything we need to know about the role each noun is playing. Look at the next sentence.

The boy gives the dog the cat.

Here, The cat is given to the dog.

There is nothing special about each word, we could exchange any of them and the meaning would change. Because in English, the word order determines what role each noun plays in the sentence. In Latin it is different, the nouns change form in order to indicate what role they play in the sentence, just like he and him.
To see how this functions, let's say the previous sentence this way:

He gives the cat to the dog.

We can switch this around in several different ways now and the meaning doesn't change:

He gives to the dog the cat.

To the dog he gives the cat.

All because of the word TO. Latin nouns function just like this, but they change the end of words. Let's go back to our first sentence:

Dog bites man.

In Latin, we essentially add an M to the end of the word serving as the object. And the subject doesn't change - it's the default or dictionary form of the noun.

So we can imagine this sentence becoming:

Dog bites manem.

And you see, we could rearrange the words anyway we want without changing the meaning.

Manem dog bites.

Bites manem dog.

13

Dog manem bites.

These would all mean the same thing. In Latin, each noun in the sentence has a different ending depending on the role it is playing.

This means that if we switch the M to dog, as in:

Man bites dogem.

then the meaning switches to the more surprising sentence: Man bites dog.

Or instead of, He gives the cat to the dog, we could imagine this as:

He gives catem dogo.

Here the M signifies that the cat is what is being given and the O on dog signifies that the cat is being given TO the dog.

This is how the nouns function in Latin, but the problem is that there are so many different endings that it takes a while to learn them all. Because not only does each noun have a gender, but there are also different classes. However, throughout this book you will acquire all these forms naturally through stories and simple sentences, which is much more fun than trying to memorize grammar tables.

LESSON 2

Let's review a little what we learned in the last lesson: Do you remember how to say, "The farmer works and sleeps"?

Agricola labōrat et dormit.

Now say, the teacher teaches and the student learns.

Magistra docet et discipula discit.

This contains the verbs from the proverb we learned:

Quī docet, discit.   He who teaches, learns.

Now try to say, You work and write and study and sleep.

Tū labōrās et scrībis et studēs et dormīs.

Did you remember that scrībis has a short I sound? Finally, what is, The student reads?

Discipula legit.

Don't worry if you didn't remember them all, we'll be reviewing them more as we go along. But if you feel unsure (or didn't get any of them), it might be a good idea to re-read lesson one. Look at the next sentence now.

Magistra discipulam docet.

The teacher teaches the student.

Do you see how discipula changed form? The subject and object of the verb have different forms so that we can tell them apart as we saw in the Interlude. The subject is the doer of the verb and this is the dictionary or default form of the verb, which we saw in the first lesson. The object is the thing the verb is being done to and in Latin we have to change the form of the verb, or decline it, in order to tell it apart from the subject. So if we want to switch the people and say, "The student teaches the teacher," we say:

noun

Discipula magistram docet.

Did you also notice that the verb comes at the end of the sentence? This is where the verb customarily goes, but actually word order is pretty flexible in Latin. Since the subject and object have different forms, we know that:

Discipula magistram docet.
     and
Magistram discipula docet.
     and
Discipula docet magistram.

Have the exact same meaning. The only difference is the emphasis: the first and last positions of the sentence are the most important, so this is where the verb usually goes.

Can you guess what the wrd "epistula" [eh-PISS-to-luh] means? If you know what an epistle is, it should be easy. Following the last example, try to say now, The poet writes a letter.

Poēta epistulam scrībit.

Since verbs conjugate differently for each subject, Latin can be a very economical language. We don't need to mention the subject if it's obvious. In fact, we shouldn't, unless we're trying to put emphasis on the subject. So these are complete sentences:

Legō.   Labōrō.   Dormiō.
I read.   I work.   I sleep.

As well as Julius Caesar's famous saying:

Venī, vīdī, vīcī.
I came, I saw, I conquered.

16

However, this is in past tense, which we won't cover for a while. And note the pronunciation, which is probably different from what you have heard. This is pronounced:

[WEN-ee WEED-ee WEEK-ee]

This second verb allows us to make much use of our new noun forms. In the infinitive it is:

vidēre [wid-AY-reh]

What does this sentence look like it means? (Remember, the Latin language died before cameras were invented.)

Poētam videō. [WID-eh-oh]

This verb has roots in the word visual and video. It has a few other meanings, but here it means "to see". So can you interpret this sentence now? I see the poet.

Do you see why it's not "the poet sees"? Because the m added to poēta signifies that it's the object. And videō is the conjugation for "I see". How would we say, "The poet sees"?

Poēta videt. [WID-et]

How about "The student sees the letter"?

Discipula epistulam videt.

Recalling that the infinitive is vidēre, how do we say, You see the teacher?

Magistram vidēs. [WID-ays]

And, you read the letter?

Epistulam legis.

Look at the next sentence. Can you guess the meaning? A hint for the last word is that the words imbibe and beverage are derived from it.

Agricola aquam bibit. [UH-kwum BI-bit]

17

That's right, this means, "The farmer drinks water."

And how would you say, "You study the water"?

Aquam studēs.

So far, Latin is pretty easy, right? If you have a large vocabulary in English, you will be able to guess and quickly learn a lot of Latin words. It helps too if you know Spanish or another Romance language. Let's ramp it up a little now.

Discipulae magistra   [dis-KIP-uh-lye]

This means "the student's teacher". The ending "-ae" is like " 's" in English. This is known as the genitive case or the possessive case.
But in Latin, we can also say,

Magistra discipulae

because word order is flexible in Latin. These two phrases have the exact same meaning. Some scholars claim the second is more common, but this topic is controversial. So we can think of this either as ""the student's teacher", or as "the teacher of the student" in order to get the order right. Note also that the diphthong "ae" in Latin is pronounced [eye], like eyeball. Try to figure out this sentence now.

Epistulam poētae legō.   [poh-AY-tai]

I read the poet's letter. Or I read the letter of the poet.

Aquam agricolae bibis.

You drink the farmer's water.   (water of the farmer)

Try this one now:

Discipula epistulam magistrae scrībit.

Did you figure it out?   The student writes the teacher's letter.

This noun declination is kind of like an adjective; however, adjectives have a different form as we will see now.

Longam epistulam scrībō.   [LONG-um]

I write a long letter.

Easy, right? We just match the ending of the adjective with that of the noun. It's not always as simple as this, though, as we'll see later. Can you guess what the next adjective means? A hint is the word magnify.

Magistra magnam discipulam docet.   [MUG-num]

Who is large in this sentence? The teacher or the student?

That's right. The teacher teaches the large student.

Now, who is large in this sentence?

Magistra magna discipulam docet.

This time it's the teacher. Word order is so flexible in Latin that adjectives can come before or after the noun, or even somewhere else in the sentence. However, outside of poetry, adjectives will usually come next to the noun they modify. But this is why declensions are so important in Latin, we can't correctly figure out the meaning if we don't pay careful attention to the declensions and conjugations.

Do you know the word pulchritude? Knowing that this means beauty will help you figure out the next new word.

Magistra magna discipulam pulchram docet.

The large teacher teaches the beautiful student.

Now, the next sentence has two new words in it, but I'm confident you can guess what they mean.

Magistra docet sed discipula nōn discit.

The teacher teaches, but the student doesn't learn.

In Latin we don't need all this "do" and "does" business from English. We just throw nōn in the sentence to negate the verb. Now what do you think the following sentence means?

Magistra docet sed nēmō discit.   [NAY-moh]

19

Did you guess that nēmō means "no one" or "nobody"?

Now we're going to read a story. That's pretty amazing after just two lessons, right? But it will be a very simple story using mostly what we've learned. There are two words you're going to have to guess the meaning of, though.

To get the first one, think for a moment what the infinitive of a verb means in English. We know what scrībō, scrībis, and scrībit mean. But what does scrībere mean? I'll give away, though, that the word "quod", means "because", since that would be hard to guess. Remember that. Quod, means because.

Magistra agricolam scrībere docet. Agricola studet et scrībere discit. Epistulam pulchram scrībit quod magistra bene docet. Agricola epistulam bene scrībit sed nēmō legit.

The teacher teaches the farmer to write. The farmer studies and learns to write. He writes a beautiful letter because the teacher teaches well. The farmer writes the letter well, but no one reads it.

Did you understand it? Kind of a sad ending, huh? Let's go through it.

In the opening sentence we have "scrībere docet", which means "teaches to write". We can use the infinitive of a verb when we want to say "to read" and "to work" etc. This is done again in the second sentence where it says "learns to write."

Then it says, "He writes a beautiful letter" and notice we don't need to add "he" here since we know the subject is the farmer. Quod means because as I said above and then we have this word "bene," which is also in the next sentence.

"Bene" is contained in the words benevolent and beneficence, so it probably has something to do with goodness or kindness. But the ending doesn't match the ending of magistra, so it's probably not an adjective but an adverb. So from the two usages, we can guess that it means "well," the adverbial form of good.

20

The last two sentences, then are "He writes a beautiful letter because the teacher teaches him well. The farmer writes the letter well, but no one reads it."

PRONUNCIATION INTERLUDE

Everyone who studies Latin should learn at least the basics of pronunciation, but how much effort you put into it will depend on what you want to do with Latin. For example, if your sole interest is in reading Latin, then this crash course is perfect for you.

One curious aspect about Latin pronunciation is that since it's a dead language, you are free to choose which era's pronunciation you would like to speak. However, this chapter will present Classical Latin pronunciation, which has come to be the standard pronunciation that people learn.

For English speakers, the pronunciation is fairly easy to master, because there are only three sounds outside of English phonology and some people just ignore these.

The consonants all sound the same as in English except for the R, which is trilled, just like the Spanish R.

The only other difference in the consonants is that the letters C and G always have a hard pronunciation like "cat" and "go". And the letter V is pronounced like a W.

This means all of our effort needs to go into the vowels. Each vowel has two pronunciations, a short and a long version, and these are usually differentiated by putting a macron, or a line, over the long version as we have seen already.

Now, the vowels might seem a little confusing at first, because English went through the Great Vowel Shift, and we now pronounce the letters for vowels a little differently than some of the other European languages. So we'll go through them one by one.

The easiest is probably O, because the long version is pronounced just like the letter: [Oh]. The short version is pronounced like the o in off. A good word to practice with is octō, which means eight and sounds like you'd expect.

As you can see, the vowels are often referred to as short and long, but they're really more different than that and it's not just the length that is different.

For the U's, the long version is like "rude" and the short is like "put". A good practice word is ūnus, which means one.   A lot of words end in "US", so it's a good idea to learn that word well.

The "I" might prove troublesome, because the long version is pronounced just like the letter E. The short version, though is the same "I" as in "sit". A good practice word is scrībit, which means he or she writes.

One note about this vowel is that when it is sandwiched between two vowels or is at the beginning of the word followed by a vowel, it is pronounced like a Y. The name Jupiter in Latin is written:

Iūppiter.   [YOOP-pit-er]

And the long version of the "E" is another difficult one because it's pronounced like the letter A. But if you know the numbers in Spanish, it's easy to remember that "three" in Latin is pronounced trēs.

The short version of "E" is pronounced like the "E" in "bet". So we can practice with bene, which means well. As in you speak Latin well. It sounds just like benefit.

And the long "A" in Latin is pronounced like the "ah" in father, but our practice word is the word for mother, or māter. The short A is like the end of idea. Practice with the most important city for Latin: Rōma.

Sometimes two vowel letters will combine into one sound. This is known as a diphthong. When A and E combine, it's pronounced "eye". This diphthong is used constantly in noun declension, for example:

Rōma → Rōmae.

The only other diphthong you'll commonly see is AU. In America, we pronounce this Aw. But in Latin it is like the beginning of the word "Ouch". It is also how Australians pronounce Australia.

One aspect of consonants that is not like English are the letter combinations ch, th, and ph. Both letters are technically supposed to be pronounced like the middle of "brickhouse" "hothead" and "uphill." If you can manage that, congratulations, but it seems like most people just pronounce them like c, t, and p. So you can practice with pulcher, theatrum, and amphora.

The final aspect we should learn is where to put the accent or emphasis. The accent always comes on either the second to last or third to last syllable. So, obviously, if the word is only one or two syllables long, the emphasis comes on the first syllable.

For words of three or more syllables, the accent always comes on the third to last syllable, unless the second to last syllable is "heavy". Heavy syllables are ones with a long vowel, so for example, this word salvēte, is pronounced with the accent on the ē.   [sal-WAY-teh]

And two following consonants can also make the second to last syllable heavy, for example,

Magistra   [ma-GIS-tra]

Let's review our practice words.

Octō   ūnus   scrībit

trēs   bene

māter   Rōma

And remember also that the letter V is pronounced like a W.

The rest of the sounds in Latin are rarer, so it's not a good use of our time to practice them until we run into a word that uses them.

LESSON 3

The nouns we have been using so far all ended in "-a", and these are typically feminine nouns. For example, Discipula and Magistra mean female student and female teacher respectively. However, in languages there are exceptions to every rule, and agricola and poeta are actually masculine nouns even though they end in -a. So, can you guess what the following means?

Discipulus studet.   [dis-KIP-uh-lus]

That's right, the male student studies. Using what you know so far, try to guess how to say, I see the male student?

Discipulum video.

Do you remember how to say the farmer reads the poet's letter?

Agricola epistulam poētae legit.

Now let's change it to the male student's letter:

Agricola epistulam discipulī legit.

The "-us" changes to "-ī".

Another pair like Discipula and Discipulus is Amīca and Amīcus. And an amicable person is someone you would call a.........friend. What does this say? (Replace the B with a V in your mind.)

Amīcum habeō.

That's right, "I have a male friend". Now say, the male student has a female friend.

Discipulus amīcam habet.

Since it was habeō with an e before the ō, we know that it's habet with an e. And what does this tell us about the case Tū (you)?

Say now, "You have the farmer's letter".

Epistulam agricolae habēs.

That's right, the "e" in habeō tells us it will be habēs with a long "e".

If you like jargon, the nouns that end in "-a" are called nouns of the first declension and the nouns that we're learning now are called nouns of the second declension. There are five declensions and there are also a few irregularities, like the following second declension noun:

Poēta librum scrībit.

Can you guess what this sentence means? A LIBRary contains many books, right? This means "The poet writes a book."

If we look at the following table, we can see that this word is regular in all but the first case, where it doesn't end in -us. This is called the nominative case because it names or nominates the noun.

Amīcus	Liber
Amīcam	Librum
Amīcī	Librī

Another regular second declension noun is Gladius. A hint to the meaning is that a Gladiātor uses this to fight with. Yes, a gladius is a sword.

Say, the male student has a sword.

Discipulus gladium habet.   [GLUH-dee-um]

Just as an illustration, can you think of how to say, "The sword's male friend?"

Amīcus gladiī   or   gladiī Amīcus

26

Both are correct. Remember, only the -us gets dropped, so it's gladiī.

And the more sensible, "male friend's sword" would be?

    Amīcī gladius   or   Gladius amīcī

Now we're going to introduce our first irregular verb. The Latin word for "to be".

    Agricola est poēta.

The farmer is a poet.

So "is" = "est" in Latin. Pretty easy to remember, right?

Note that both nouns are in the nominative case. The "to be" verb is like an equal sign, Agricola = poēta, so both nouns are in the same case. Now, this is also often written Agricola poēta est, because the verb usually comes last.

When talking about our friends, we don't usually say, "The student is friend." We add the word "my." When we want to add this word in Latin, though, it has to be declined, just like an adjective.

So the female student is my friend would be:

Disicupla est amīca mea.

And the male student is my friend would be:

Discipulus est amīcus meus.

Do you remember how to say "beautiful"?
Try to say, "The teacher is beautiful."

Magistra est pulchra.   or   Magistra pulchra est.

Because est is like an equal sign, the adjective matches the noun. So when we have a male noun, pulchra will change form. But it declines like liber not amīcus. Thus, "the male student is beautiful" is:

Discipulus pulcher est.

It's a little strange, but adjectives decline according to the gender of the noun, not necessarily the nouns ending. So, recalling that Poēta refers to a male, how would we say the poet is beautiful.

Poēta pulcher est.

And the same would go for Agricola. Do you remember the word for big? It declines just like amīcus. Try to say, the farmer is big.

Agricola magnus est.

The Latin for "you are" is "Tū es". Say to a woman now, "You are a student".

Tū es discipula.

Did you remember to match the gender of the noun to the "you" in the sentence?

dup. ✗ Did you remember to match the gender of the noun to the "you" in the sentence?

Say to a man, now, "You are the male student's friend."

Amīcus discipulī es.

Remember, the words can come in any order, but for the sake of time I'll only give one combination.

And "I am" has yet another form in Latin:

Ego sum.

Say I am a big student.

Magnus discipulus sum.

If you're a male, and if you're female:

Magna discipula sum.

The genders make it a little difficult, but after a while they will come naturally.

Now, if you have the potential to do something, then you are able to or can do it.

In Latin, this is pot plus the verb for "to be".

possum	I can
potes	You can
potest	He/she/it can

Can you see the forms of "to be" attached to this verb? Note that the t changes to s in the first person case, so it is possum, not potsum. Let's try to use this now to say, the poet can write well. Think back to the story from the last lesson.

Poēta bene scrībere potest.

Do you remember how to say, But no one reads it?

Sed nēmō legit.

Now say, My friend can't read.

Amīcus meus nōn potest legire.

The following word came to English from French instead of Latin, but it's still easy to see the connection between desire and dēsīderāre. This word means desire, want, and to miss someone, among other things. What does this mean?

Amīcum dēsīderō.

I desire a friend.

And for the next story, we will need the word for girl, which is puella. Leaving the word for "he" unstated, say, "He desires the girl."

Puellam dēsīderat.

Now say, "The poet is not a girl."

Poēta puella nōn est.

And now try, You read the girl's letter.

Epistulam puellae legis.

Did you get the endings right? Now we're ready for this lesson's story. However, this story is a little longer and will be concluded in the next lesson. In this story, we'll also see a preview of what's to come in the following lesson, but you'll be able to guess the meaning of these words.

Also, Jupiter is the name of Zeus in Latin. And Europa was one of the many human girls he chased after.

Iūppiter et Eurōpa

Iūppiter est deus et in Olympō habitat. Terram spectat et puellam Eurōpam videt. Eurōpa pulchra est et Iūppiter puellam dēsīderat. Iūppiter sē in taurum trānsfōrmat quod Eurōpa est timida.

Jupiter and Europa

Jupiter (Zeus) is a god and lives in Olympus. He watches the earth and sees the girl Europa. Europa is beautiful and Jupiter desires the girl. Jupiter transforms himself into a bull because Europa is timid.

Were you able to guess the meaning of this first sentence? It means "Jupiter is a deity and lives in Olympus". "Habitat" should be pretty obvious from the words habitat and inhabit. And can you guess the meaning of the word "terra" from the English word subterranean? It means earth.

"Spectat" is what a spectator does, so "terram spectat" means "watches the earth". Then we see the sentence we just learned "puellam dēsīderat".

But did you note something weird? The name Europa conjugated! That's right, names in Latin conjugate just like every other noun.

This little word sē in the next sentence means "himself/herself/oneself, etc." It's a reflexive pronoun, but don't worry about it for now, that's a more advanced topic.

But did you guess what a taurus is? This is one of the constellations, represented by a bull. And do you remember this word "quod" from the last story? It means because, so this last sentence can be translated, "Jupiter transforms himself into a bull because Europa is timid".

It's pretty convenient that we could guess about one third of the words in this story from English, isn't it? We'll see how this story ends in the next lesson.

LESSON 4

In the previous lesson's story, we encountered "in Olympō" but we know that the home of the gods was called Olympus, right? This ō ending is another noun declination called the ablative. The name is not important; what we need to remember is that we use this form when we talk about the location of an action. (There are also a few other uses, some of which we'll cover in the next few lessons.)

Olympus is a regular male noun just like Amīcus, so how would we say, in the friend?

in amīcō

And try to say god of Olympus.

Deus Olympī

I'm sure you've heard this phrase, although probably with a different pronunciation.

In vīnō vēritās.   [in WEE-noh WAYR-ih-tas]

In wine, there is truth.

Can you spot what's missing from this sentence?   The word est.

But because it's obvious, it isn't needed and the sentence has a better ring without it. (This is technically called ellipsis.) Here again with vīnō we have the ablative. However, the nominative case for wine is actually vīnum. This is our first neutral noun. Neutral in the sense of neither feminine nor masculine. Do you remember what the verb drink is in Latin? Here's how to say, "I drink wine".

Vīnum bibō.
Neutral nouns are the same whether they're the object or the subject.

However, since neutral nouns are inanimate objects, this doesn't get confusing because we know that "Vīnum bibit" cannot mean "the wine drinks" It has to be referring to an unstated pronoun like he or she.

Do you remember what the name Pennsylvania means? This means "Penn's woods". So what do you think the following sentence means?

Vīnum in silvā bibis.   [SIL-wah]

You drink wine in the forest. (It's better to use the word forest since it's singular)

Looking at the ending of the word, can you guess how to say, The forest is large?

Silva magna est.   [SIL-wuh]

This noun declines just like discipula.

If you know the words amble, ambulatory, and perambulate it will help you remember the next word.

In silvā ambulō.   [UM-bu-loh]

This means, I walk in the forest. As in, the forest is the location that I am walking around in. If we change the declination of silva, we can change the meaning to that of entering.

In silvam ambulō.

I walk into the forest.

Does it make sense? Here the forest is the object of the verb, just like with epistulam scrībō. So it is the objective, or aim of the movement. Whereas with the ablative case "in silvā" we are referring to the location of the movement. And we actually saw this form in the last lesson's story in the sentence:

Iūppiter sē in taurum trānsfōrmat

33

We can see now why this means transforms INTO a bull and not inside a bull or something like that. In the last story, we also saw the word meaning to live or reside in some place, i.e. to inhabit. Can you remember how to say, "God lives in Olympus".

Deus in Olympō habitat.

We can see now why this means transforms INTO a bull and not inside a bull or something like that.

In the last story, we also saw the word meaning to live or reside in some place, i.e. to inhabit. Can you remember how to say, "God lives in Olympus".

Deus in Olympō habitat.

And now, if you know that the verb is ambulāre, you can say, The god walks into Olympus. But try to make it a female god this time.

Dea in Olympum ambulat.

Have you heard the phrase "ad nauseam" as in he rambled on ad nauseam. Can you see from the second word that this phrase comes from Latin? Ad is another preposition like in, and nausea is declined with an "m" just like "In silvam." This means literally "to the point of seasickness." (The root nau refers to the sea, as in nautical.) We can use this phrase to remember how to say, "You walk to the forest". Try to guess how to say it.

Ad silvam ambulās.

If something is PORTable, you can...carry it, right. Another word containing this root is transPORT. Here is how to say the Farmer carries water.

Agricola aquam portat.

Can you think of how to say "The bull carries the girl"?

Taurus puellam portat.

Remember this sentence, because it will appear in this lesson's story. Let's make a longer sentence: "You carry the letter to the forest."

Epistulam ad silvam portās.

And "I carry a book and wine into Olympus."
Librum et vīnum in Olympum portō.

Let's pause to review the noun declensions we've covered so far:

Puella	Gladius	Liber	Vīnum
Puellam	Gladium	Librum	Vīnum
Puellae	Gladiī	Librī	Vīnī
Puellā	Gladiō	Librō	Vinō

The first column are nouns of the first declension and they are all feminine nouns except for a few like agricola and poeta. The other three columns are all second declension nouns, the first being the regular declension masculine nouns and the last being the regular declension for neutral nouns. Note, though, that the declensions are thankfully all the same in these columns except in the nominative case.

And the first-declension nouns are not that different from them. All the nouns end in an M in the second row, in the third row we have the sounds ae and ī, which are similar, and in the last row we have long vowels.

It's important to really build a strong foundation with these cases so that we don't get bogged down with the rest of the declinations, because there are still three more declinations and also plurals. If you're feeling uncertain, it might be good to review the previous lessons; otherwise, let's break into some plural forms.

In the next sentence, there is a new word and a new verb form.

Discipulus et discipula in scholā student.

Because we are talking about two students, the verb changed from studet to student. It's that easy, we just add an "n". And you guessed what scholā means, right? And you know what declension it is? Say I walk to school.

Ad scholam ambulō.

Let's go back to our students now.

Discipulae in scholā student.

Wait, what? We already saw this form and it was used for saying things like the student's book. Well, it's also the plural form. And oddly, the plural form in English adds an s and the genitive form, as in student's book, adds an apostrophe s. So we can use this fact to help us remember that these two forms are the same. Can you think of how to say, The farmers work?

Agricolae laborant.

Now try to say, the female students see the poet's letter.

Discipulae epistulam poētae vident.

Can you see that this sentence is ambiguous? It could also mean The poets see the female student's letter. With isolated sentences like this, we can only guess the meaning; it is only when we have a larger context that the ambiguity dissolves.

To figure out the next sentence, recall that a fugitive is someone that flees:

Puellae fugitant.   [FUG-ih-tunt]

The girls flee.

Now try to say, the girl flees to the forest.

Puella ad silvam fugitat.

The next word doesn't have a strong connection to its English meaning, except that they share many letters. The word "insula" means "island". It might help to think that an island is INSULAted.
Let's say, "The farmers carry a book to the island."

Agricolae librum ad insulam portant.

And before we finish the story from the last lesson, let's review one of the words we encountered, since it will also be in today's story.

✗ And before we finish the story from the last lesson, let's review one of the words we encountered, since it will also be in today's story. Do you remember how to say, "watches the earth" or "looks at the earth"? The two words had connections to spectator and subterranean.

terram spectat

How would we say, I don't look at the letter.

Epistulam nōn spectō.

There's just one more word we need to know for this lesson's story: Nunc, which means now.

And as a reminder, in the story Jupiter was trying to woo Europa and changed himself into a bull.

Iūppiter et Eurōpa (cont.)

Eurōpa taurum spectat et taurus puellam portat. Nunc puella nōn est timida. Taurus fugitat et Eurōpam ad insulam Crētam portat. Deus et puella in insulā habitant.

Jupiter and Europa (cont.)

Europa looks at the bull and the bull carries the girl. Now the girl is not timid. The bull flees and brings Europa to the island Crete. The god and the girl live on the island.

The first sentence is pretty straight-forward: she looks at the bull, then is carried by the bull or mounts it. Now she is not timid. But then the bull flees and takes her to Crete.

And do you see, here we have the form "ad insulam", because the bull carries her TO the island of Crete. Then in the next sentence we have "in insulā", with the ablative, because the island is the location where they are living. And the story ends with a plural verb, which we'll be dealing with more in the next lesson.

LESSON 5

The last lesson covered a lot of new material, so let's review a little. Do you remember what the following phrase means?

Discipulī et discipulae in scholā student.

The male students and female students study in school.

Both the verb and the two types of students are plural. And scholā is in the ablative form. Now try to say, "The farmers walk".

Agricolae ambulant.

Did you put both words in plural form? The next one's a little harder. Can you think of how to say, "The gods live in Olympus"?

Deī in Olympō habitant.

When the group is all men or mixed, we use the male plural form. But for example, if we are talking about a group that is all female, as in "The female friends flee", we would say:

Amīcae fugitant.

Can you remember the Latin word for "to read"? It conjugated a little bit differently than the other verbs. It was Ego legō, like leggo my Eggo and then Tū legis followed by legit.

39

For the plural, we can't just add an N, we have to switch the vowel to U, so "The poets read" is:

Poëtae legunt.

We learned three other verbs that conjugate like this, can you recall them?

The first is related to read, because before you can read a letter, someone has to ___ it?

Yep, say "the male students write a letter".

Discipulī epistulam scrībunt.

Try to remember that: for reading and writing we have "it" and "unt".

And the second was in the proverb we learned. He who teaches... Say "the female students learn".

Discipulae discunt.

So, of the verbs we've learned so far, the ones that are connected to studying we have to study a little more: reading, writing, learning. And the final verb is the other thing students often do: drink.
Say, the girls drink.

Puellae bibunt.

"We" is also a plural form and also gets it's own conjugation. But it's really easy to remember, because "We walk" is: Ambulāmus. Do you see the connection? We – us AmbulāmUS

Verbs conjugated in We-form always end in "mus". Say now, We walk into the forest.

In silvam ambulāmus.

The Latin word for "we" is nōs. Notice that we have tū ambulās and nōs ambulāmus. The vowel before s and mus is the same. Do you remember how to say, "You drink"?

Tū bibis

Say now, "We drink in the forest" (and this time use the word for we):

Nōs in silvā bibimus.

Because it's tū bibis, we have Nōs bibimus. And how would we say, The poet and I read?

Poēta et ego legimus.

Do you understand why we used legimus instead of legunt? Because the subject included ego.

"Via" means "road" in Latin. We travel VIA road. And to deviate is to depart from the established course. Let's say now, "The road is long".

Via longa est.

Now we'll change it to the plural form.

Viae longae sunt.

Every word changed form! But you expected that, right? Because both the adjective and the verb have to match the noun. And from this we see that the plural of est is sunt. Similar to scrībunt and bibunt. We will see this word so much, that you'll have no trouble remembering it, so don't worry.

Let's learn another proverb.

Omnēs viae Rōmam dūcunt.

This first word means "all", it is the plural form of omnis, which sometimes combines with words to make compounds like omnipotēns, or all-powerful, and omnivorus, eats everything.

And I'm sure you can guess the meaning of Rōma, so in this sentence we have "All roads" and something to do with Rome. Do you recognize the proverb?

All roads lead to Rome.

So the verb dūcunt means lead, just like an air duct leads air to each room and to deduce is to bring to a conclusion.

And think about the verbs discunt and legunt for a moment. How would we say, "The road leads to Rome"?

Via Rōmam dūcit.

Because it's discit and legit.

Notā bene: notice that we used Rōmam by itself. Certain places don't require a preposition and Rome is one of them. But we conjugate it in the accusative form, because it's the object or aim of the verb.
The next sentence is a gimme.

Rōma in Ītaliā est.

Rome is in Italy. Hopefully you knew that. But with Italy, we used IN plus the ablative, just like in silvā. Using this, say Italy is in Europe.

Ītalia in Eurōpā est.

Now comes the crazy part.

Romae habitō.

I live in Rome.

This is neither the possessive form nor the plural form. There is yet another form that shares the same "-ae" ending!

This is called the locative case, because it tells where something is located. Most nouns don't have this case, but you need to be aware of it so that you don't get confused. Because there is yet another case that shares the same "-ae" ending!

This more common case is known as the Dative case and it indicates the indirect object of the verb or the recipient of the verb. If you remember from the Grammar Interlude, this was the "dogo" case, meaning "to the dog." Let's explore this case some more.

Poēta agricolae legit.

The poet reads to the farmer.

The farmer is the recipient of the reading.

However, because multiple cases share the same ending, such short sentences can be ambigious. Can you see it? The word agricolae could also be in the genitive case and the sentence would mean: The farmer's poet reads. Here's another ambiguous sentence:

Poēta agricolae epistulam legit.

This can mean either, "The poet reads the letter to the farmer".
"The farmer's poet reads the letter".
Or: "The poet reads the farmer's letter".

The fact that some of the cases are the same can get a little annoying, but usually the context makes the meaning clear. Nevertheless, this is probably the hardest part about reading Latin.

A better verb for demonstrating the dative is the word "to give". This verb is "dare" in Latin and is a little bit irregular, as we can see by the fact that the infinitive is dare and not dāre.

Let's try this verb with the dative declension for a male noun.

Discipula discipulō gladium dat.

The female student gives a sword to the male student.

Dropping "-us" and adding "-ō" gives the dative form for masculine nouns. Can you remember what declension this is the same as? It matches the ablative form, so this too can be ambiguous. We really have to have context when deciphering Latin, because so many of the forms match. Can you figure out this sentence?

Magistrō tunicam das.

You give the male teacher a tunic.

We have to pay attention to conjugation and declension in this sentence, since the verb "das" indicates that the subject is an unstated "tū" and not the first word in the sentence.

And do you remember that we learned Magistra before? That was the feminine form of the word, "Magister" indicates a male teacher and declines just like "Liber".

So it is Magister in the nominative form, but all other declensions drop the E, so we have Magistrum, Magistrī, Magistrō, etc.

Notā bene: the conjugation for "you give" is "das" with a short vowel, just like "dare". In the present tense, this verb always has a short vowel, which is what makes it slightly irregular.

Using this fact, try to say, "We give the girl water". (And use the word for we.)

Nōs puellae aquam damus.

Did you remember that the conjugation contains "US"? Can you figure out the meaning of the next sentence?

Optimus sum, quod possum legere.

I am the best, because I can read.

Optimal is obviously related to optimus, we just have to remove the "al" and add the Latin endings to use this word. How would you say this sentence if you're a woman?

Optima sum, quod possum legere.

Two more words will be briefly introduced for this lesson's story, and used more in later lessons:

Amīcum volō.   [WALL-oh]

I want a friend.

This verb doesn't have a direct English connection, but perhaps saying volōnteer will help you remember it. Because you volōnteer for things you want to do. Another example is:

Nunc scrībere volō.

✗ Now I want to read. write

And the other word we need is in this sentence.

Hīc labōrō.

44

I work here.

Also, the various forms of the verb "to be" can also mean, there is, there are, etc. For example,
Hīc sunt librī.

There are books here.
Or the much cooler.

Hīc sunt dracōnēs.

Here be dragons.

There are a few other new words in this lesson's story, but they resemble their English counterparts so closely that I'm sure you can understand them. Let's go!

Rōma

Rōma optima est. Viae Rōmānae dīrēctae sunt et aqua clara est. Hīc tunicae pulchrae sunt et arma splendida sunt. Volō hīc habitāre.

Rome

Rome is the best. The Roman roads are straight and the water is clear. Here there are beautiful tunics and the weapons are magnificent. I want to live here.

The first sentence is easy to understand. In the second we have, Viae Rōmānae dīrēctae sunt. Viae is the plural form of "via" and Rōmānae is the genitive form, so this means Rome's streets, or streets of Rome.

And dīrēcta obviously means direct, or in this case straight. So we have the streets of Rome are straight.

And did you guess what clara means? The sentence is talking about good qualities of Rome and says the water is...clear. Clara = clear.

Then we have the new words "arma splendida". The second is obvious, and

45

you can probably guess that the first means arms, as in weapons, so we have "the arms are splendid".

And in the final sentence we have the two words we just learned. Notā bene: The two verbs are placed first and last to place emphasis on them, like saying, I WANT to LIVE here.

LESSON 6

In order to review, let's first learn a simple question.

Quid facis?

Based on what we've learned, we can already guess two things about this question. The first is that quid is a Wh-question word, just like quī, which we saw in the first proverb. And the second word looks like a verb conjugated for "tū". The keyword to help you understand this verb is FACtory, because it means "do" or "make".

And if you haven't guessed it, this question is, "What do you do?" or "What are you doing?"

Latin doesn't distinguish between these two forms, because there is no "-ing" conugation in Latin.

Can you guess how to ask, "What is the male student doing?"

Quid discipulus facit?

Try to say, "Now he is reading." (Remember, you don't need to say he.)

Nunc legit.

Legit can mean either he reads or he is reading, depending on the context.

Now ask, "What is the male teacher doing? " (Remember, this was a weird noun.)

Quid magister facit?

Answer, "He is teaching."

Docet.

It's crazy how economical Latin is, right? Let's change it up a little.

Ask now, "What is the female student reading?"

Quid discipula legit?

Easy right? Now be careful with the answer. Say, A letter.

Epistulam.

Did you remember the M? Even though we're omitting half the sentence, the words still need to be declined in the proper form.

Can you remember from the last lesson's story how to say, "Rome is the best"?

Rōma optima est.

It's like saying Rome is optimal.

Not all question words begin with a QU. Try to guess the meaning of the next sentence.

Ubi est Rōma?

Where is Rome? Something that is UBIquitous is found everyWHERE. Try to ask now, "Where do you live?"

Ubi habitas?

How about, "Where is the farmer working now?"

Ubi agricola nunc labōrat?

It's a little easier than English, since we don't need to rearrange the words as much. And do you remember what the next sentence means?

Volō hīc habitāre.

I want to live here.
The verb meaning "to want" is irregular. Try to guess the meaning of the next sentence.

Ubi habitāre vīs?

Where do you want to live?

For yes/no questions, we simply add the suffix "-ne" to the first word in the sentence. For example:

Studesne?   Dormisne?

Are you studying? Are you sleeping?

Try to ask, "Are the students drinking wine?"

Discipulīne vīnum bibint?

We also add a rising intonation at the end of the sentence as well as "-ne". It's kind of convenient that "-ne" comes first, though, since it indicates that the sentence is a question. This way you're not surprised at the end of the sentence.

We can also start the sentence a little bit differently. Look at the next sentence.

Nōnne agricolae labōrant?

This "nōnne" is a combination of the word "nōn" and the suffix "-ne" that we just learned. Adding it to the sentence is like asking, "The farmer's are working, no?" Or: "The farmer's are working, aren't they?" Sometimes it's also translated as "Surely the farmer's are working?"

Ask, "You're reading the book, aren't you?"

48

Nōnne librum legis?

One way to say yes in Latin is:

Ita est.

"Ita" means "so", so this literally means, "It is so". Kind of cool, huh? In the next sentence, I'm sure you can figure out the new word from context.

"Ita est," dīcit agricola.

Yes, says the farmer.

The words diction and dictate are derived from this word. We will start seeing this now in the stories when there is quoted speech.

Let's review giving and the Dative case now by introducing a new declension:

Mīlitī aquam dō.

I give the soldier water. Or: I give water to the soldier.

You can see the connection to "military", right? It's not so clear, though, in the nominative case, for example:

Mīles agricolae gladium dat.

The soldier gives the farmer a sword.

This word is our first third-declension noun. Beyond the first-declension, the declensions become more annoying, because the nouns are more irregular and there is overlap among the endings.

For example, when we say "to the soldier," we use the form Mīlitī. Can you remember what discipulī means?

Adding "-ī" to second-declension nouns (like discipulus), is like adding an s or an apostrophe 's. So it signifies the plural or the possessive as in "students" or "student's".

And how do we say "to the male student"?

discipulō

49

So for the Dative case, we have:

agricolae discipulō mīlitī

Another third-declension noun is Fēlis. Do you recognize this word? The word Fēlis is where we get the term feline. Remember this word for the story.

Here's a sentence with only third-declension nouns:

Mīles fēlī carnem dat.

The soldier gives meat to the cat.

Can you see the connection between carnem and carnal? They both carry the meaning of flesh.

Now say, "I give the book to my friend". ("My" is understood.)

Amīcō librum dō.

We will look at one more third-declension noun in this lesson, because it will be in the story. The word "mūs". This is another animal that has a connection with fēlis. It's a....mouse, right? But when it's an object it changes to this:

Fēlis mūrem edit.

The cat eats the mouse. (Don't worry, they'll be friends in the story.)
Let's try to say, "We eat and drink".

Nōs bibimus et edimus.

We're ready now for this lesson's story. However, there is one word you might not be able to guess. The word deinde means, "then", or "after that". It's used often in stories for narrating sequential events, so we're going to be seeing it more now in the stories.

Fēlis et Mūs

Fēlis ad silvam ambulat quod amīcum dēsīderat. "Nonne hīc sunt amīcī," dīcit et in silvam ambulat. Fēlis mūrem videt et mūs fēlem spectat. Deinde

50

mūs fugat. Sed fēlis celer est et mūrem cōnsequitur.

The Cat and the Mouse

A cat walks to the forest because she desires a friend. "Surely there are friends here," she says and walks into the forest. The cat sees a mouse and the mouse looks at the cat. Then the mouse flees. But the cat is fast and chases the mouse.

Did you guess the last word? It has many meanings, but here it means "chase". We can remember it by thinking, consequences chase our actions, or follow them closely. Okay, we'll see what happens with the cat and mouse in the next lesson.

LESSON 7

The third-declension nouns are pretty complicated, so let's review what we learned about them. In the story we had the sentence:

Fēlis mūrem videt et mūs fēlem spectat.

For almost all third-declension nouns, they always end in "-em" when serving as the object. We can see this also in the next sentence:

Mīles fēlī carnem dat. This sentence also shows the dative case, or the recipient, which is indicated with an "-ī: ending. (And as was mentioned in the last lesson, this ending indicates a different case than the same ending on second-declension nouns.) Thankfully the genitive case is different as we can see in the next sentence.

Fēlis cibum mūris edit.

The cat eats the mouse's food. The word cibum means food. It might help to think of the word kibble, the hard dog and cat food, in order to remember this word. And looking at the ending, what declension is it?
Second. Which means the nominative form is "cibus".

Let's compare the three declensions.

Nom	Magistra	Cibus	Fēlis
Acc	Magistram	Cibum	Fēlem
Gen	Magistrae	Cibī	Fēlis
Dat	Magistrae	Cibō	Fēlī
Ab	Magistrā	Cibō	Fēle

Thankfully there are not too many repeated endings, but regrettably it's the two most complicated cases, the genitive and the dative, that contain the overlap. And this list doesn't include plurals, which contain more repeated endings.

For this reason, it's better to slowly introduce the declensions, rather than try to memorize tables when studying Latin.

And it gets worse when we add pronouns, because these have their own pattern. Look at the next sentence:

Dominus mihi cibum dat.

The first word obviously has a connection with "dominate" and has meanings like master or lord. And you may have guessed that the second word is the pronoun meaning "to me".

So this sentence means, "The master gives food to me". And this sentence?

Tibi librum dō.

I give the book to you.

They're only connected by one letter, but tibi is the dative form of tū.
Do you remember the second word in this sentence?

Servus meus es.

From the word servus, we derived the word servant, but in Latin it can also have the meaning of slave. So this sentence means, "You are my slave". Kind of scary. And there is also a poem by William Butler Yeats titled,

Ego dominus tuus.

I am your lord. Or: I am your master.

And what's another way we could say this?

Dominus tuus sum.

Try to say now, I am not your slave.

53

Nōn servus tuus sum.

The verb "laud", as in "to praise", comes directly from the Latin word "laudāre". So say now, "The master praises the slave."

Dominus servum laudat.

The word "rarely" is "rārō" in Latin, say now (with all male forms), "The teachers rarely praise the student."

Magistrī discipulum rārō laudant.

Say, "I rarely praise you".

Tibi rārō laudō.

And try to say now, "The soldier rarely gives the cat food".

Mīles fēlī rārō cibum dat.

To understand the next sentence, recall that when you are enAMOred, you are in love.

Linguam Latinam amō.

I love the Latin language. (Or just Latin.)

And you understand Lingua, right? We use this word in bilingual and lingua franca. Let's make it plural now.

Poēta linguās amat.

The poet loves languages.

Pretty convenient that the plural involves an "S", right? Not also, that the "A" became long, because the nominative case is just lingua.

Recall that in the story we had "Mūs fēlem spectat." and try to guess now how to ask, do you love cats?

Fēlēsne amās?

Did you remember the "-ne"? For second-declension nouns, the vowel changes. We have:

Magistra discipulōs laudat.
The female teacher praises the students. Say now, The female student loves books.

Discipula librōs amat.

Let's pause for a moment to take this in. When a noun serves as the object of the verb, or is in the accusative case, it ends in an "-m" when it's singular and an "-s" when it's plural! For all five declensions! There are a few exceptions, but that makes it so much easier to decipher Latin, doesn't it? If only the other cases were so easy...

The next new word we'll need for the story, but it's also really convenient. It's the way to say, "Don't"

Nōlī aquam bibere.

Don't drink the water.

Notice that the verb is in the infinitive form when we use the word "nōlī". But that makes some amount of sense, right, because there isn't really a subject in the sentence.

For the next sentence, recall that in order to say "my", we say "me-" plus the appropriate ending for that noun. Try to say, Don't read my letters.

Nōlī epistulās meās legere.

But remember that the adjective declines according to the gender of the noun, so they don't always match. For example, Cat is feminine in Latin, so we have.

Omnēs fēlēs meās amant.

Everyone loves my cats. Another word that will be in the story is at the end of this sentence.

"Nōlī cibum meum edere!" mūs clāmat.

Did you guess the meaning? Don't eat my food, the mouse exclaims.

It's like making a clamor with your voice, so it can mean exclaim, scream, cry out, etc. And we will also see "edere" in various forms throughout the story, so remember its meaning! Let's go!

Fēlis et Mūs

"Nōlī fugere!" fēlis clāmat. "Amīcum volō!"
"Fēlis et mūs amīcī nōn sunt!" clāmat mūs. "Quod fēlēs mūrēs edunt."
"Nōn mūrēs edō, quod dominus mihi cibum dat." dīcit fēlis.
"Nōn mūrēs edis?" rogat mūs.
"Ita est," dīcit fēlis. "Sumusne amīcī?"
"Ita est," dīcit mūs.

Cat and Mouse

"Don't run away!" the cat cries. "I want a friend!"
"A cat and mouse are not friends!" the mouse cries. "Because cats eat mice."
"I don't eat mice, because my master gives me food," says the cat.
"You don't eat mice?" asks the mouse.
"That's right," the cat says. "Are we friends?"
"Yes," says the mouse.

There was one word that we hadn't learned yet, but I'm sure you guessed that "rogat" means "asks". It has roots in "interrogate", but this will be easy to remember as we'll see it more in the coming lessons.

LESSON 8

For this lesson, we're going to do something a little different. We're going to go through the Lord's Prayer in Latin line by line and learn to read it (the full text is at the end of this chapter). If you are familiar with the text, you should be able to learn from it very rapidly.

This text will help us learn a new aspect of verbs: mood. The easiest to understand is the imperative mood. This is used when we make requests, demands, commands etc. For example, saying "Give me money". The other mood is called the subjunctive and has too many different uses to cover in one chapter, but the use we will see here is like saying, "May the Force be with you". It is similar to a command, but there is uncertainty of whether it can be carried out. Let's compare:

You give me money.	Indicative.
Give me money.	Imperative.
May you get lots of money.	Subjunctive.

This is a really difficult concept for English speakers to grasp, which is why I thought it best to introduce it through this familiar text. But remember it's not something that you can learn from reading one chapter; this is just a warm-up.

The first line of the prayer starts out easy:

Pater noster, quī es in caelīs,

The word Pater is very close to Father, right? This follows exactly the sound change denoted by Grimm's Law, which states that p's change to f's and t's to

57

th's. This law was actually conceived by Jacob Grimm of the Brother's Grimm who first presented this sound change systematically and is interesting to read about if you're into language origins.

And do you remember how to say, We? Nōs. So "Pater noster" means.... Our Father.

Now, from what you've learned in the previous lessons, you can probably guess that the rest means, "who is in heaven". But there's a little twist. Since we are talking about where he is located, we should use "in+ ablative", right? Caelum is a second-declension noun, so the ablative form is caelō. But this prayer uses the plural ablative form, caelīs. So this line is really, Our Father, who is in the heavens.

The next line is:

sānctificētur nōmen tuum,

This doesn't seem so foreign to us now, does it? The words "nōmen tuum" are obviously your name, nōmen is related to nominate, but the tuum is deceptive, because nōmen is a third-declension neutral noun.

Remember how vinum was the same in both the nominative and accusative form? Tuum is the same when modifying a neutral noun: the nominative and accusative form are the same. So nōmen tuum could be either the subject or object.

Now, we know that this means, "Hallowed be your name," which is passive, but to understand the Latin better, let's think of it as, "May your name be sanctified," because it's a <u>subjunctive-passive</u> form. This means though that "nōmen tuum" is the subject, because in passive sentences, the noun being acted upon becomes the subject.

For example, in active sentences, we say, "The police arrested the thief". But the passive would be, "The thief was arrested by the police". And "the thief" is now the subject of the sentence.

The subjunctive is easy to form for verbs that end in -"are", we switch the "A" to an "E" and add the normal ending.

So instead of sānctificat it's sānctificet. However, sanctificō becomes sanctificem, since the first-person case doesn't really have an ending.

58

Then, as you can see, to form the passive we just add the suffix "-ur" for the third-person. We won't go into the other cases here, but just know that **if a verb ends in "R", then it's in passive form**. (99% of the time)

The third line is:

Adveniat rēgnum tuum.

We know that verbs in the indicative mood can only end in "-at", "-et", or "it", so this must be another subjunctive form.

This verb is advenīre, so the rule for this case is we switch the "I" to an "IA" and add the normal ending. The English word advent is derived from this, so advenīre means to arrive.

And the second word, rēgnum, gives us regency, regicide, and reign in English and means kingdom or reign. So this line means, "May your kingdom arrive". We continue with:

Fiat voluntās tua

We know that volō means I want and if you recall, the way to remember this was that we Volōnteer for the things we want to do. Voluntās is a third-declension noun meaning the things we want to do, or our "will".

And from "tua", we can see that this is a feminine noun and since "tua" is the nominative form, we know that "fiat" is a passive verb. This is actually the word we learned in the question, "Quid facit?"

So what would the subjunctive be?

Faciat.

Sadly, though, this verb is irregular in the passive form, so instead of *faciatur, it becomes:

Fiat.

And what did "Quid facit?" mean?

What are you doing?

So this line means, "May your will be done".

59

Okay, we made it through the hardest part!
The next line is easy:
sicut in caelō, et in terrā.

The only new word here is "sicut", which means "just like" or "as". There isn't a trick for this word, it just has to be memorized. And notice that now the word for "heaven" is singular.

Pānem nostrum quotīdiānum da nōbīs hodiē,

Here is our first imperative form. In the lessons we used dat, das, and dō, but here we see just da. The imperative is really easy, just subtract the "-re" from the infinitive and you've got it! So already we can say,

"Da!" = "Give!"
"Scrībe!" = "Write!"
"Labā!" = "Work!"
"Lege!" = "Read!"

In the line above, in front of "da", we see three words ending in "m", so we know these things are what is being demanded. Pānis is bread, another third-declension noun. It might help to remember this by thinking the bread is in the PANtry. And "nostrum" is obviously the accusative form of "noster".

The next word we actually also have in English, "quotidian", which means "daily". It's like "a day quota". So this first part means, "give our daily bread".

Then we have "nōbīs" and since this starts with "NO", you can probably guess that it has something to do with "we". This is the dative pronoun, so it means "to us". Remember, we use the dative case to indicate who is the recipient of the giving. And hodiē is a combination of hōc + diē or "this day".

et dīmitte nōbīs dēbita nostra

"Dīmitte" means "dismiss". It's as if someone who just had a Novocaine injection is trying to say the word. ;)

And "dēbita" is also exactly what it sounds like: debts.

These two words of course have other meanings and here they are being used figuratively. As you would expect now, "nostra" is also just another form of

60

"noster", it's the plural neutral.

So this phrase means, "Cast away from us our offenses".

There are a lot of similar words in the next sentence:

sicut et nōs dīmittimus dēbitōribus nostrīs.

Here is the word "sicut" again, which means "just like" or "as". And now the word for dismiss is conjugated for We. Remember, verbs end in "US", when conjugated for We. Now dēbita has changed to dēbitōribus. This is the dative plural form of dēbitor, which means debtor, just as you'd guess.

And as you certainly also guessed, nostrīs is the dative plural form of noster.

So this line means, "Just as we cast away from our offenders". (The object is left unstated since it is the same as the previous line.)

The next line is very close to English:

Et nē nōs indūcās in tentātiōnem,

The word "nē" usually indicates that a subjunctive verb is coming. It negates the verb just like "nōn", but with a subjunctive verb it has a meaning more like, "That you not".

"Indūcās" is the subjunctive form of "indūcere". Note that the vowel changed to a long "A". It's similar in meaning to induct, meaning "lead into" or "introduce".

And note that tentātiōnem is the accusative form, not ablative, so it means, INTO temptation. Altogether then this means, "And lead us not into temptation".

The final line is also very close to English:

sed līberā nōs a malō.

Another imperative form: līberāre obviously means "liberate" or "free". And the root "MAL" is in many English words like malevolent, malicious, etc., meaning "evil". So we end with, "But liberate us from evil".

And here's the full text:

Pater Noster

Pater noster, quī es in caelīs,
sānctificētur nōmen tuum,
adveniat rēgnum tuum.
Fiat voluntās tua,
sicut in caelō, et in terrā.
Pānem nostrum quotīdiānum da nōbīs hodiē,
et dīmitte nōbīs dēbita nostra,
sicut et nōs dīmittimus dēbitōribus nostrīs.
Et nē nōs indūcās in tentātiōnem,
sed līberā nōs a malō.

The Lord's Prayer

Our Father, who is in Heaven
may your name be glorified.
May your kingdom come;
may your will be done
on earth as it is in heaven.
Give us our daily bread today.
And forgive us our offenses,
as we forgive those who offend us.
And don't allow us to fall into temptation,
but liberate us from evil.

LESSON 9

In this lesson we'll play a little more with one of the new verb forms we learned. The <u>imperative mood</u> is often used when giving directions.

Now the word for "turn", is contained in the English word, "genuflect". This literally means "bend the knee".

So we have "Genū" which means "knee" and "flectere", which means "bend". And how do we turn this into a command?

Flecte

Bend or Turn

Do you remember how to say, "The farmer walks TO the forest".

Agricola ad silvam ambulat.

We learned this word from "ad nauseum". Or to the point of sea sickness. So can you guess what this means?

Flecte ad sinistram.

Turn to the left. And this would be?

Flecte ad dextram.

Turn to the right.

These words came to English with slightly different meanings and the etymology is unclear, but if you're right handed, you can remember them easily by thinking something like, My right hand is dextrous, but my left hand does sinister things when I try to use it.

How would we say, the soldier turns to the left.

Mīles ad sinistram flectit.

And here's the plural form:

Mīlitēs ad dextram flectunt.

Say now, "Read the book".

Librum lege.

This has the short form of "I", but in Pater Noster, there was a very similar word in the line, "Liberate us from evil".

Do you remember how to command, Liberate? Or even the whole line?

lībera

And the full line was:

Līberā nōs a malō.

This word has the long version of "I". And there is also an adjective, līber, which means things like "free" and "independent".

So we could actually say, "Liber līber", which depending on the context could mean something like "Independent book" or "unbiased book". But these words show why it's important to pronounce the vowels correctly, since they might take on a totally different meaning.

The way to say Go home is:

Domum ī.

Can you see the connection between domus and domicile? The verb īre on the other hand doesn't have a connection to English and is mostly irregular; however, in the present tense it is regular except for first person and third-

person plural.
Here is the first-person case:

Domum eō.

I'm going home.

Two lessons ago we learned how to say, "The master praises the slave". Can you remember what it was? One of the words was similar to "Domus".

Dominus servum laudat.

And you've probably seen or heard this phrase:

cum laude

It means with honors or praise.

The preposition "cum" requires the noun to be in the ablative form. We're going to learn to say now, "Go with Julius please".

Cum Iūliō ī, quaesō.

We saw once before that names decline in Latin and here Iūlius has changed to Iūliō because it's a male name.

Quaesō is the way to say please in Latin, but this is not another ablative form, it's a verb, meaning literally, "I beg". If you know that cheese is queso in Spanish, then you can think Cheese, please. Queso Quaesō. ;)

Let's say now, "The poet and the male student go".

Poēta et discipulus eunt.

This was the other irregular form in present tense. Try to change it now to "The poet goes with the male student".

Poēta cum discipulō it.

Notice that the verb became singular, just like in English.

Try, "The cat walks with the farmer".

Fēlis cum agricolā ambulat.

The greeting "Salvēte" that opened the book is actually also an imperative form. But it's plural. The "-te" on the end is a pluralizing suffix and we simply add this to the normal imperative form to make it plural in all but one case. The verbs that end in "-ere", but switch to "I" in second person also switch to "I" in the imperative plural form.

For example, scrībere becomes scrībite. So really, to form the plural imperative, we use the "Tū" form and replace the "S" with "TE". Say now in plural form, Study!

Studēte.

Learn!

Discite!

Drink wine!

Vīnum bibite!

In the last lesson, we learned the word Pater, so let's add some other familial words to our vocabulary.

Māter fīliam amat.

The mother loves her daughter.

Māter is easy and we also have the word filial in English, as in filial love – the love of a child for a parent.
And if daughter is "fīlia", guess what son is.

Fīlius

And guess what this means: Iūlius duōs fīliōs habet.

Julius has two sons. Remember the "-ōs" is the accusative male plural.

Duo is the number two in Latin and we'll need another number for the story. Can you figure out the meaning of this? It's the title of a famous fairy tale about animals that try to build houses:

trēs parvī porcī

66

The three little pigs.
Porcī is pretty easy to remember, no? And if you know how to count to three in Spanish, then you already know the word for three in Latin.

The word "parvus" is a little difficult to remember, and there's no help from English because it's only used in obscure medical terms. It might help to associate it with puny or petty, but you're best bet to remember it is just to repeat the phrase: "trēs parvī porcī".

The following is another world we'll need for the story, but is also very important. The following sentence means, "It's a small world".

Mundus parvus est.

You can remember the word "mundus" with the phrase "mundane world" and if you've seen too much of the world, everything becomes mundane. And if I mention that the final word in the next sentence is related to "edifice", but is a verb, can you guess what the next sentence means?

And if I mention that the final word in the next sentence is related to "edifice", but is a verb, can you guess what the next sentence means?

Lingua mundum aedificāt.

Language builds the world.

The prefix "EX" can be added to the verb "īre" to make a new word. So in the third-person it is "exit", which means.... "goes out" or "leaves". Even though this verb contains the prefix "EX", it often uses this as a preposition, or when followed by a consonant "ex" becomes "ē".
For example,

Ē culīnā exī!

Get out of the kitchen.

Culīnā is obviously associated with culinary. But what case is this noun?

Ablative

Try to read this sentence.

Volō tē ē domō meā exīre.

I want you to leave my house.
Did you notice something weird? "Domus" is a feminine noun! It's actually even weirder because it has a mix of fourth- and second-declensions as well as a locative case. But we'll encounter this word several times in the following story, so don't worry.

The final word we'll learn for the story is "Cavēte". This means, "be careful" or "take care". Notice that it's the plural imperative. If we want to say it to one person we say, "Cavē". Notice that the emphasis shifts with and without the TE.

Cavēte   [ca-WAY-te]
Cavē   [CA-way]

We're now ready for the story of trēs parvī porcī. The only word you might not be able to guess is "strāmentum", which means "straw". The other new word I'm sure you can guess.

Trēs Parvī Porcī

Sunt trēs parvī porcī et in mundum exīre volunt. "Cavēte," dīcit māter et prīmus porcus parvus exit. Domum aedificāre vult. Agricolam videt et dīcit, "Dā mihi strāmentum, quaesō." Et prīmus porcus parvus domum suam aedificat.

The Three Little Pigs

There are three little pigs and they want to go out in the world. "Take care," says their mother and the first little pig leaves. He wants to build a house. He sees a farmer and says, "Give me some straw, please." And the first little pig builds his house.

I'm sure you guessed that "prīmus porcus parvus" means "the first little pig". That's one difficult aspect about numbers: not only do you have to learn one, two, three, and so on, but also first, second, third, etc.

Fortunately, they're not so foreign, they start out:

prīmus, secundus, tertius, quārtus.
And could you guess what word ended this sentence?

Domum aedificāre vult.

This is the third-person conjugation of volō, "I want." So this sentence means, "He wants to build a house."

LESSON 10

Let's review:
How did we say, "Turn to the right".

Flecte ad dextram.

And, "I'm going home"?

Domum eō.

And how would we say, "I want to go with Julius"?

Volō cum Iūliō īre.

Remember, word order is flexible in Latin, so there are other alternatives. And what did the following sentence mean?

Ē culīnā exī!

Get out of the kitchen!

We can use the following construction to ask permission to do something: "licetne mihi". We already know two parts of this. Remember the "-ne" is used attached to the first word in the sentence when we ask yes/no questions. And "mihi" is the dative form of "Ego", meaning "for me". "Licet" means "it is allowed", or "one is permitted". So literally this means, "Is it permitted for me...?" But a better translation is, "May I". Look at the following sentence.

Licetne mihi domum īre?

May I go home?

Notice that the word for "go" is in the infinitive. Can you figure out what this means?

Licetne mihi ad lātrīnam īre?

May I go to the bathroom?
And in the story, we will see this:

Licetne mihi intrāre?

What English word does "intrāre" sound like?

Enter.

This means, "May I enter?" or "May I come in?"

Remember Julius Caesar's famous phrase:

"Venī, vīdī, vīcī".

The first two words are "I came, I saw". And we already learned that the second one in present tense is videō. The first word in present tense is veniō = "I come".

Do you see the connection to GO?
This word is venīre = ven+ īre. It contains īre. What does the following sentence mean?

Potesne venīre?

Can you come?

Remember, we say what our POTential is, or "what we can do", by adding "pot" to the appropriate form of "to be". Say now, "I can come".

Possum venīre.

Look at the following sentence:

Hīc venī, amīce.

Come here, friend.

"Amīce" is yet another declension, but this one is much easier to understand. It's called the Vocative form, because we're inVOKing a person or thing. We don't have an equivalent in modern English, but it's like saying, "O Romeo." Or in this case, O friend.

I mentioned before that in Shakespeare's play, Julius Caesar says, "Et tu, Brute?" as he is dying. This is the vocative form of Brutus. So this is like saying, "You also, O Brutus?"

And in fact, the greeting "Salvēte omnēs." that opened the book also contains a vocative form. Omnēs is the vocative form of omnis, a third-declension noun. One thing that makes the vocative form much easier is that the vocative form is the same as the nominative form for all but words that end in "-us".

See if you can say, "Soldier, turn to the left".

Mīlēs, ad sinistram flecte.

That one was kind of hard, but notice that the vocative form is the same as the nominative.

Keeping in mind that amīcus becomes amīce, how would we say, "Little pig", using this form.

Parve porce

Obviously this will also be in the story. Look at the next sentence:

Agricola gladium dēlet.

The last word looks just like the English word "Delete", but it means "destroy", which has a somewhat similar meaning. So this sentence means, "The farmer destroys the sword." And this sentence?

Puella mala epistulam dēlet.

The bad girl destroys the letter. Say, "I destroy the big book."

Librum magnum dēleō.

Here's a famous phrase that you'll want to memorize if you want to sound

72

smart. ;)

Cōgitō, ergō sum.

We have a similar word to the first one in English: "cogitate", which means "to think deeply", or "reflect". We already know the last word, so can you guess what this famous phrase is? "I think, therefore I am." This is the famous statement of Rene Descartes. And we can see that "ergō" means "therefore".

Here is another famous logical statement from philosophy (and it's filled with third-declension nouns):

Omnēs hominēs mortālēs sunt.
Sōcratēs homō est.
Ergō Sōcratēs mortālis est.

This is a syllogism meaning,
All men are mortal.
Socrates is a man.
Therefore Socrates is mortal.

So we see that homō and hominēs mean man and men.

The next phrase also has a recognizable word.

Nihil cōgitās.

You don't think about anything.

And this phrase might also be recognizable:

Lupus ululat.

The wolf howls.

You've heard the term "Canis lupus", right? This is the scientific classification for wolves. And "ululate" is an English word meaning "howl". Say now, "The wolf eats the pig."

Lupus porcum edit.

We're now ready for the story, but there will be several words you will have to guess. However, remember that "deinde" means, "then".

Deinde magnus lupus malus domum porcī videt. Lupus venit et dīcit, "Parve porce, parve porce, licetne mihi intrāre?"
"Nūllō modō!" prīmus porcus parvus clāmat.
Ergō magnus lupus malus inhālat et exhālat et domum dēlet. Deinde magnus lupus malus parvum porcum edit.

Then the big bad wolf sees the pig's house. The wolf comes and says, "Little pig, little pig, may I come in?" "No way!" cries the first little pig. So the big bad wolf inhales and exhales and destroys the house. Then the big bad wolf eats the little pig.

Did you understand the first sentence? "Magnus lupus malus" means "the big bad wolf". And then "domum porcī" means "the pig's house". Remember the "-ī" is added to masculine nouns with the meaning " 's". So this first sentence means, "Then the big bad wolf sees the pig's house."

Then we have the words, "Nūllō modō", which I'm sure you guessed was some kind of rejection. Nūllō means "not any", just like the word "null" in English. And modō is the ablative form of "modus", as in modus operandī, "the method or way of doing something". So this phrase simply means, "No way!"

And "inhālat et exhālat" clearly mean "inhales and exhales".

There's more to this story coming in the next lesson.

LESSON 11

Do you remember how to say, "The big bad wolf"?

magnus lupus malus

We can just sandwich the noun between the two adjectives.

But adjectives change form when the gender changes. Say, "The bad girl destroys the letter."

Puella mala epistulam dēlet.

We also learned the vocative declension. Say, "Come here, friend".

Hīc venī, amīce.

And what was the famous phrase of Rene Descartes?

Cōgitō, ergō sum.

Finally, can you say, "The second little pig"?

Secundus porcus parvus   [se-CUN-dus]

Because secundus has a double consonant, the stress comes on the second syllable. Double consonants make the preceding vowel "heavy". Look at the next sentence.

Servus lignum colligit.

75

The slave collects wood.

"Colligit" means "collect" and sounds very similar.

"Lignum" can mean "firewood" or just wood in general. This is a second-declension noun and as you would expect, neutral, just like vīnum; so the nominative, accusative, and vocative forms are all "lignum". To help you remember this word, lignin is the material that makes plants more rigid.

A really cool suffix that we can use in Latin is "-eus". This is similar to our suffix "-eous" as in "gaseous" or having the characteristic of gas. But the suffix in Latin can be used to mean "made of." For example, "ligneus" means "made of wood." This is an adjective, so the feminine form would be?

Lignea.

And remember, the word for house in Latin is actually a feminine word, even though it looks and declines like a masculine one. So how do we say, "A house made of wood".

Domus lignea

The word for stone in Latin is "lapis", but the root is really lapid. This is where we get the word lapidary in English, a person who cuts and polishes gems. So if the root is lapid, how do we say, "made of stone"?

lapideus

Let's try to say now, "The slave collects wood and builds a house made of wood".

Servus lignum colligit et domum ligneam aedificat.

Try now, the master lives in a house made of stone.

Dominus in domō lapideā habitat.

Don't worry if you don't get every declination correct on the first try. They take a long time to master. Just make sure you understand why a certain declination is used in each situation.

For example, here we say "domō", which is the ablative, because it is the location where the living is done. It's a static action.

However, when movement is involved, we use a different declination. How do we say, "The mother enters the house".

Māter in domum intrat.

And do you remember what the following means?

Pater cum filiō in silvā ambulat.

The father walks around in the forest with his son.

Here the ablative is used with the two nouns because "cum" always triggers the ablative and "in silvā" is indicating the location of the movement. So even though they're moving around, their movement is located in the forest. Do you remember how to say, "Get out of the kitchen!"

Ē culīnā exī!

This is another example where a preposition triggers the ablative, like cum. So even though movement is involved, the ablative is used. It's annoying, I know, but there are exceptions to every rule in languages. Keeping this sentence in mind, look at the next one:

Servī domum ē lignō aedificant.

So we have, "The slaves build the house", but what does "ē lignō" mean?

Out of wood.

"Ē culīnā" = "out of the kitchen"
"ē lignō" = "out of wood"

If you're familiar with the story of the three little pigs, then you know this will be in this lesson's story.

For the story, we also need to know a very useful adverb. The next sentence contains the word "also". Can you understand it?

Tūne quoque Rōmae habitās?

Do you also live in Rome?

The word "quoque" means "also". And remember, Rōma is kind of weird and doesn't need the preposition "in" because it has a locative form.
Say now, "I am also a student".

Ego quoque discipulus sum.

If you're male. And

Ego quoque discipula sum.

If you're female.

We don't necessarily need to say "Ego", but it adds a little bit of emphasis. Look at the next sentence.

Habēsne līberōs?

This actually means, "Do you have children?" But it refers to the children of free people, ie., those who were not slaves. Recall that līber means free and it's easy to see the connection to līberī in the nominative and līberōs in the accusative.

Answer: "Yes, I have a son. I have a daughter, too."

Ita est, filium habeō. Quoque filiam habeō.

Remember also that the words we learned for "book" and "free" and now "(free) children" are very similar. Which is which between these two sentences?

Habēsne līberōs?

Habēsne librōs?

The first means, "Do you have children?" and the second means, "Do you have books?"

The story will be longer this time because some of it will be review. But before we begin it, try to recall what these two phrases meant:

Nūllō modō

Licetne mihi

The first means "No way!" And the second, "May I...?"
Okay, let's read the story.
Secundus porcus parvus quoque domum aedificāre vult.
"Cavēte," dīcit māter et secundus porcus parvus exit. Silvam videt et lignum colligit. Deinde porcus parvus suam domum ē lignō aedificat.
Nunc magnus lupus malus venit et domum ligneam videt. Lupus dīcit, "Parve porce, parve porce licetne mihi intrāre?"
"Nūllō modō," secundus porcus parvus clāmat. Ergō magnus lupus malus inhālat et exhālat et domum ligneam dēlet. Deinde magnus lupus malus parvum porcum edit.

The second little pig also wants to build a house.
"Take care," says their mother and the second little pig leaves. He sees a forest and collects wood. Then the little pig builds his house out of wood.
Now the big bad wolf comes and sees the house made of wood. The wolf says, "Little pig, little pig, may I come in?"
"No way!" cries the second little pig. So the big bad wolf inhales and exhales and destroys the house made of wood. Then the big bad wolf eats the little pig.

LESSON 12

In the last lesson we learned two very similar questions. Do you remember how to ask, "Do you have books?"

Habēsne librōs?

And the other similar question was. "Do you have children?" What was it?

Habēsne līberōs?

Remember this refers to the children of "free" people, hence the connection to līber, free or independent. And how did we say, "Do you also live in Rome?"

Tūne quoque Rōmae habitās?

And do you remember how to say, "Out of wood"?

ē lignō

In this lesson's story, the house will be built out of stone, so we need to know "ē lapide". Adding an "-e" is how we decline the ablative form for third-declension nouns. So this sentence is now obvious:

Porcus parvus suam domum ē lapide aedificat.

The little pig builds his house out of stone. And how do we say, "House made of stone"?

domum lapideam
Do you remember how to say, "Cat and cats".

Fēlis et fēlēs

Try to say now, "The daughter collects stones".

Fīlia lapidēs colligit.

Can you figure out the next sentence now? The second half is a hint.

Fīlius ad montem it et lapidēs colligit.

The son goes to the mountain and collects stones.

A new adjective we need for the story is "callidus". This means smart, wise, clever, etc. It doesn't have a connection to any English words, but maybe you can remember it by thinking, The smart person tells US what everything is CALLID (= called). ;)

Look at the next sentence.

Quālis canis callidus!

What a clever dog! The word "Quālis" can be used to say, "What a..." or "such a..." or can also be used to ask, "What kind of..."

Quālis arbor est?

What kind of a tree is that?

Keeping in mind that vivacious means "lively" and "felicity" and "intense happiness", what do you think this sentence means? (It will come at the very end of our story.)

Trēs parvī porcī fēlīciter vivunt.

The three little pigs live happily. There are two common words for to live in Latin:
"Vivire" means "To live one's life"
and the other is:
"habitāre", which is more like to "inhabit".
What does the next sentence mean?

81

Vive et disce.
Live and learn.

These are both in imperative form.

But how do we say, "I want to live in Italy"?

Volō in Ītaliā habitāre.

And try to guess what this sentence means.

Arborēs in summō monte sunt.

There are trees on top of the mountain.

The word "summus" sounds a lot like the English "summit", right? And "summō" and "monte" are in the ablative form since we are speaking of where the trees are.

Recalling that the verb "iterate" means "to perform again and again", look at the next sentence.

Iterum autumnus est.

It is autumn again. "Iterum" is an adverb meaning again. And this?

Tempta iterum.

Try again.

You can remember this first word by associating it with "attempt". The next sentence means The dog jumps.

Canis salit.

This has a tenuous connection to the word "assault". It might help if you recall that "to jump someone" is a colloquial way to say assault someone. And in the next sentence, they're jumping into a body of water. What do you think it means?

Omnēs in lacū saliunt.

82

Everyone jumps in the lake. The next sentence should be easy.

Amīcus meus īrātus est.
My friend is irate. (Or angry).

Remember, the verb "to be" is like an equal sign, so the adjective has to have the same form and gender as the subject. So try to say now, "My mother is angry".

Māter mea īrāta est.

And how would we say, "The girl is smart"?

Puella callida est.

The counterpart to "puella" is "puer", which means boy. This is a second-declension noun and it conjugates just like liber. (Unlike with discipulus, it's like the "-us" got removed in the nominative form. So instead of puerus it's just puer.) Try to say now, the boys are smart.

Puerī callidī sunt.

And how would we say, "The boys and girls are irate"?

✗ And how would we say, "The boys and girls are irate"?

Puerī et puellae īrātī sunt.

Because it's a mixed group, the adjective conjugates in the plural male form.

This contains some words we learned a while ago, but do you remember how to say, "The farmer can work"?

Agricola labōrāre potest.

And what about the male teacher flees.

Magister fugit.

We're ready now for the conclusion of Trēs Parvī Porcī.

Trēs Parvī Porcī (fīnis)

Tertius porcus parvus quoque domum aedificāre vult sed callidus est.

"Cavēte," dīcit māter et tertius porcus parvus exit. Ad montem it et lapidēs colligit. Deinde porcus parvus suam domum ē lapide aedificat.

Nunc magnus lupus malus venit et domum lapideam videt. Lupus dīcit, "Parve porce, parve porce licetne mihi intrāre?"

"Nūllō modō," tertius porcus parvus clāmat.

Ergō magnus lupus malus inhālat et exhālat sed domum nōn dēlere potest. Lupus clāmat et inhālat et exhālat iterum et prīmus et secundus porcus ē lupō saliunt! Nunc lupus īrātus est et fugit.

Et trēs parvī porcī fēlīciter vivunt.

Did you understand what ē lupō saliunt means? "Jumps out of the wolf."

The Three Little Pigs

The third little pig also wants to build a house, but is smart.

"Take care," says their mother and the third little pig leaves. He goes to the mountain and collects stones. Then the little pig builds his house out of stone.

Now the big bad wolf comes and sees the house made of stone. The wolf says, "Little pig, little pig, may I come in?"

"No way!" cries the third little pig. So the big bad wolf inhales and exhales, but can't destroy the house. The wolf screams and inhales and exhales again and the first and second pig jump out of the wolf! Now the wolf is angry and flees.

84

And the three little pigs live happily.

LESSON 13

In this lesson we will take a different approach than before. We will START with the story, because at this stage you will probably be able to understand most of the new words without help. But I will add some explanations along the way.

Hic est Maximus. Puer est. Hic puer discipulus est. Maximus est discipulus bonus.

Haec est Valentina. Puella est. Haec puella quoque discupula est. Valentina est discipula bona.

Hīc sunt Maximus et Valentina. Hic est Maximus. Maximus est frāter Valentinae. Haec est Valentina. Valentina est soror Maximī. ✗ ?

Ok, hopefully you understood frāter and soror. These are contained in the words fraternity and sorority. And we learned "bene" before, which means "well", the adverb form of "good". So "bonus" and "bona" mean...good.

The other thing we have to notice is that "hīc" is completely different from "hic". Hīc means "here". It's an adverb that doesn't ever change form.

"Hic" and "haec", on the other hand are demonstrative pronouns that have to decline. These can mean "this" or "these". But they refer to things near the speaker. There are other words that refer to things near the listener, and yet more words that refer to things far away from both. And they all have to match gender. So when we speak about masculine nouns, we have to use hic.

86

And when we speak about feminine nouns, we have to use haec. There is also a neutral version, hoc, which can also be used to refer to things in general. For example, what does this mean?

Hoc edite.

Eat this you guys.

And we also use it when we don't know the gender.

Quid hoc?

What is this?

Hopefully you also noticed the dative form in the two sentences:

Maximus est frāter Valentīnae. Valentina est soror Maximī. ✄ ᷲ

It's like saying Maximus is the brother to Valentina. And Valentina is the sister to Maximus. Let's continue with the story.

Quis est haec? Haec fēmina est māter. Octavia est. Maximus est fīlius Octaviae. Valentina est fīlia Octaviae. Octavia māter Maximī et Valentinae est. Māter fīlium et fīliam amat.

Pater Maximī est Augustus. Augustus fortis est. Agricola est et in agrō lābōrat. Maximus patrī similis est. Valentina mātrī similis est. Octavia pulchra est. Ergō Valentina pulchra est. Maximus dīcit, "Soror mea pulchra est. Et māter mea quoque pulchra est."

Did you understand "fortis"? To FORTify something is to strengthen its defenses. Also, one's "forte" is one's strong point. This word means "strong".

And "similis" means "Is similar," so as you can see, we need to use the Dative case to say what the subject is similar TO. Patrī and mātrī are the dative forms of pater and māter, which are third-declension nouns. Remember, we use the Dative form when we say to whom we give something and here it's to whom one is similar.

And where does a farmer work? On the farm or in the field. So this is what "in agrō" means.

Let's see now if you can remember the new words. Try to say, "This is my brother. He is strong."

Hic frāter meus est. Fortis est.

Now say, "I look like my father."   Or alternatively say, "I look like my mother."

Patrī similis sum.
Mātrī similis sum.

Try to say now, "This is Valentina's brother."

Hic frāter Valentinae est.

And now, "This is Maximus' sister."

Haec soror Maximī est. ✗ ō

And do you remember, "Here be dragons?"

Hīc sunt dracōnēs.

And let's recall the word for "good". How do we say, "Maximus is a good boy"?

Maximus puer bonus est.

And what was the word for "woman"? It's almost exactly the same as a related English word. Say, "You are a good woman".

Fēmina bona es.

Here is the story in its totality, along with it's English translation:

Maximus et Valentina

Hic est Maximus. Puer est. Hic puer discipulus est. Maximus est discipulus bonus.

Haec est Valentina. Puella est. Haec puella quoque discupula est. Valentina est discipula bona.
Hīc sunt Maximus et Valentina. Hic est Maximus. Maximus est frāter Valentinae. Haec est Valentina. Valentina est soror Maximī.

Quis est haec? Haec fēmina est māter. Octavia est. Maximus est fīlius Octaviae. Valentina est fīlia Octaviae. Octavia māter Maximī et Valentinae est. Māter fīlium et fīliam amat.

Pater Maximī est Augustus. Augustus fortis est. Agricola est et in agrō lābōrat. Maximus patrī similis est. Valentina mātrī similis est. Octavia pulchra est. Ergō Valentina pulchra est. Maximus dīcit, "Soror mea pulchra est. Et māter mea quoque pulchra est."

Maximus and Valentina

This is Maximus. He is a boy. This boy is a student. Maximus is a good student.

This is Valentina. She is a girl. This girl is also a student. Valentina is a good student.

Here are Maximus and Valentina. This is Maximus. Maximus is Valentina's brother. This is Valentina. Valentina is Maximus' brother.

Who is this? This woman is a mother. She is Octavia. Maximus is Octavia's son. Valentina is Octavia's daughter. Octavia is Maximus' and Valentine's mother. The mother loves her son and daughter.

Maximus' father is Augustus. Augustus is strong. He is a farmer and works in the fields. Maximus is similar to his father. Valentina is similar to her mother.

Octavia is beautiful. Therefore, Valentina is beautiful. Maximus says, "My sister is beautiful. And my mother is also beautiful."

LESSON 14

In this lesson, we will begin to tackle the past tense. Just like in English, there are two different types of past tense in Latin, but they're different from English. They're called the Imperfect and Perfect tense.

The Perfect tense refers to actions that were **completed** in the past. And the imperfect refers to **continuous actions** and **habitual actions** in the past. But don't worry so much about what that means for now. Do you remember how to say, "The farmer works in the field"?

Agricola in agrō labōrat.

Now here's the past tense.

Agricola in agrō labōrābat.

To form the imperfect, we slip a "BA" in front of the T and lengthen the "A" before the "BA".

labōrat → labōrābat

Every verb follows this pattern, which means that every verb in the imperfect past tense conjugates just like "-are" verbs as you can see in the following table.

-bam	labōrābam
-bās	labōrābās
-bat	labōrābat
-bāmus	labōrābāmus
-bant	labōrābant

Since this is the imperfect tense, it signifies that the action is incomplete. So the sentence:

Agricola in agrō labōrābat.

Can mean either, "The farmer used to work."
Or, "The farmer was working." (Up until the present.)
Try to say now, "I used to live here."

Hīc habitābam.

And what does this sentence mean?

Gladium habēbam.

I used to have a sword.

Do you see what happened here? Habēre gets a long "E" before the "BA". And scrībere has a short E, but it still gets a long E in the imperfect past tense. So what does this mean?

Epistulās scrībēbās.

You used to write letters.

And verbs with a long I, like dormīre, also get a long "E", but they also keep a short "I"!

Discipulī dormiēbant.

The students were sleeping.

The context, or sometimes just the meaning, will make it clear whether to use "Used to sleep" or "were sleeping."

And how would we say, "I used to read books"?

Librōs legēbam.

Here is the imperfect conjugation for each verb form.

amāba-	habēba-	scrībēba-	dormiēba-
amābam	habēbam	scrībēbam	dormiēbam
amābās	habēbās	scrībēbās	dormiēbās
amābat	habēbat	scrībēbat	dormiēbat
amābāmus	habēbāmus	scrībēbāmus	dormiēbāmus
amābant	habēbant	scrībēbant	dormiēbant

As you would expect, the verb "to be" is irregular in the past tense, but not terribly so. It's just "ER" followed by the conjugation we just learned. So it's:

"to be"

eram
erās
erat
erāmus
erant

This is much easier than the present tense. The imperfect of "to be" is used for descriptions, because we consider that they continue over a period of time or into the present and hence are incomplete. If you add the prefix "IN" to the second word, you may be able to guess the next sentence.

Poēta ēbrius erat.

The poet was inebriated.

How would we say, "Were you shy"?

Erāsne timidus?

And in the story, we will see the following sentence:

Ōlim corvus erat.

Ōlim is the Latin version of "Once upon a time". And "corvus" is the Latin for "crow" or "raven" and hence is the name of their genus in English. We will use crow, since it's closer to corvus. So this means, "Once upon a time, there was a crow."

And as a reminder, when we say what we can do, or have the potential to do, we add POT to the appropriate conjugation of the Latin for "to be". So this sentence means:

Discipulus nōn legere poterat.

The male student wasn't able to read. (Or could not read.)
And try to say, "I could not sleep."

Dormīre nōn poteram.

Look at the next sentence.

Corvī volāre poterant.

Crows can fly.

The word for fly is a little strange, because "I fly" is volō. This is the same as the word for "I want". The rest of the conjugation is different, though, so we only have to be careful about the first-person case. But we will see both words in past tense in the story. Try to say, "The crow flew."

Corvus volābat.

And what does this mean?

Porcus volāre volēbat.

The pig wanted to fly.

One way to tell these apart is that a VOLAtile substance sends parts of itself flying out and a beneVOLEnt person wants to be kind. So volābat is the past tense of to fly and volēbat is the past tense of to want.

Another word we will need for the story is "satis". If you are SATISfied, you have enough. The word satis in Latin means "enough".

Now, if we want to say, "Enough water", in Latin, we can't just use word order as you may have guessed. But if we say, "I have enough of water" that seems to mean the same thing as "I have enough water". And remember, the genitive can mean both John's book or Book of John. So how would we say enough water (enough of water)?

Satis aquae
Aquae is the genitive form of Aqua. (And also the dative and plural if you recall.) And can you guess what the second word means? (Look at the first five letters.)

Satis temporis

Enough time.

The TIME signature in music tells you the TEMPO. The stem is "tempor", but the nominative form is "tempus". So how do we say, "Time flies"?

Tempus volat.

Virgil said the same thing but with the words:

Tempus fugit.

There is another similar statement:

Tempus volat, hōra fugit.

Time flies, the hour flees.

We don't actually use the word Tempus when we ask what time it is. If you know a romance language this should be familiar, but in Latin we ask:

"Quota hōra est?"

What time is it? Or literally, What hour is it?

We will also need to know the following word for the story: Vās, which means vase, or vessel. And note also that this word has the same nominative and accusative form. They are both "Vās". For the story, we will also need to understand the following phrase:

✗ For the story, we will also need to understand the following phrase:

Dum volābat, corvus vās vīdit.

Let's break this down: Dum means while. And "vīdit" is the perfect past tense of videt. We will be covering the perfect past tense in later lessons, but we need to introduce this word to demonstrate this construction.

In this type of sentence, the verb that interrupts the other verb is in the perfect tense, because it happens once – it's the complete action. And the continuous verb – the one that gets interrupted – is in the imperfect tense.

So this phrase means, "While it was flying, the crow saw a vase."
Ok, Let's start this story now adapted from Aesop's fables.

Corvus et Vās

Ōlim corvus erat. Et hic corvus aquam bibere volēbat. Dum volābat, corvus vās vīdit.

Erat aqua in vāse. Sed satis aquae nōn erat et corvus nōn bibere poterat.

The Crow and the Vessel

Once upon a time, there was a crow. And this crow was thirsty. While it was flying, the crow saw a vase.

There was water in the vase. But there was not enough water and the crow could   not   drink.

LESSON 15

Let's review the imperfect past tense.
How do we say, "I used to write letters"?

Epistulās scrībēbam.

And You used to read books.

Librōs legēbās.

Can you remember what this sentence means?

Dum volābat, corvus vās vīdit.

While it was flying, the crow saw a vessel.

Here the perfect tense is used to interrupt the ongoing imperfect tense. The conjugation for the perfect tense is more difficult to learn than the imperfect because it has its own pattern. Therefore we're going to take this tense slowly. Look at the next sentence.

Vīnum bibī.

Remember bibō means "I drink", so try to associate the long O with the long I of bibī.

So this means I drank wine. And remember, the perfect tense refers to past actions that were completed at one time. How would we say, "I drank enough"?

Satis bibī.

Remember, if you're satisfied, you've had enough. Here's another conjugation.

Nimis bibistī.

You drank too much.

"Nimis" means "too much" or "excessively". It kind of looks like numerous, if that helps you remember. And the word for "you drank" is bibistī. Similar to the present tense, this contains bibis and then we add tī so we can tell it apart from the present.

But then here's something weird: we can't tell the difference between the perfect past tense and the present tense for the third-person conjugation. They are both "bibit". Latin relies heavily on context. However, the third-person is only the same for certain verbs as we'll see. So what are the two meanings the next sentence could have?

Quid bibit?

What did he/she drink? Or: What is he/she drinking?

Now say, "I am reading a book".

Librum legō.

The past tense for this verb changes a little: the stem becomes "lēg", with a long "E". So say now, "I read a letter".

Epistulam lēgī.

And do you remember how to ask, "What are you doing"?

Quid facīs?

Here is the past tense now:

Quid fēcistī hodiē.

What did you do today?

We saw this word hodiē in Pater Noster and the perfect past tense of facīs uses the stem "fēc". This is what's hard about the perfect past tense: there are several different patterns of conjugation. Thankfully, though, all verbs use the same endings, so, once we learn these, we will always be able to identify a verb in the perfect past tense when we're reading or listening.

In English, we actually have the word "frangible", meaning fragile, which might help you learn this word: "frangere", which means "to fracture or shatter". So what does this mean?

Nōn vās frangere poterat,

He couldn't break the vase.
And here's the reason:

quod nimis firmus erat.

Because it was too strong.

The word "firmus" can mean things like "firm, strong, steadfast", etc. This full sentence will be in the story. T

he word "calculus" in Latin means both "calculation" and "pebble". The connection is that they used the small pebbles on the abacus to count. And this is a second-declension noun, so how do we say, "He saw pebbles"?

Calculōs vīdit.

In the next sentence, the first word contains the prefix "post-" and means "finally" or "at last".

Postrēmō calculōs vīdit et problēma solvit.

Finally it saw some pebbles and solved the problem. The second half is easy, right? It's practically the same as English. And notice that we don't need to say the word "some" since it is understood from context in Latin.

How do we say, "Come here"?

Hīc venī.

This can also mean I came here.

Try to say now, "Nobody came."
Nēmō venit.

And this can also mean nobody is coming.

We can add the prefix "per-" to this word, to give it the meaning of "doing something completely". And what does "come completely" mean?

To arrive or reach.

Remember, something that is PERmanent remains completely. And when you PERmute two things, you completely swap one thing for the other. Try to say now, "I arrived today."

Hodiē pervenī.

And in the story, we will see the following sentence:

Aqua ad summum pervēnit.

This is talking about the water in the vase. And do you remember that "summus" means "the top" or "summit". So this means "the water reached the top". Look at this sentence now.

Calculōs in aquam posuit.

If you "pose" something, you "put" it somewhere. "Posuit" is the past tense of "he or she put". So this means, "He put the pebbles in the water". (Aqua is accusative because there is movement involved.)

Finally, in the story, you will see consecutive sentences starting with these three words:

Prīmō   Deinde   Dēnique

We already know that deinde means "then" and you may be able to guess that Prīmō means "first". Dēnique is used to say "and then", or "finally". So we can see that these words are used to narrate a sequence of events.

Corvus et Vās

Nōn vās frangere poterat, quod nimis firmus erat. Postrēmō calculōs vīdit et problēma solvit.

Prīmō corvus calculōs ad vās portāvit. Deinde in vās posuit. Dēnique aqua ad summum pervēnit et corvus bibere poterat.

The Crow and the Vessel

It could not break the vase, because it was too strong. Finally, it saw pebbles and solved the problem.

First the crow carried the pebbles to the vase. Then it put them in the vase. Finally, the water reached the top and the crow could drink.

Did you notice there was an additional pattern in the word portāvit? There are a lot of different forms in Latin, but the best way to acquire them is through lots of repetition through comprehensible input. That's why I teach through stories and lots of example sentences, because "we don't learn languages, we get used to them."

FULL STORIES

Quī docet, discit.

He who teaches, learns.

Chapter 2 Story

Magistra agricolam scrībere docet.   Agricola studet et scrībere discit.
Epistulam pulchram scrībit quod magistra bene docet.   Agricola epistulam
bene scrībit sed nemo legit.

Ɏ The teacher teaches the farm to write. The farmer studies and learns to write.
He writes a beautiful letter because the teacher teaches well.   The farmer
writes the letter well, but no one reads it.

Iūppiter et Eurōpa

Iūppiter est deus et in Olympō habitat. Terram spectat et puellam Eurōpam videt. Eurōpa pulchra est et Iūppiter puellam dēsīderat. Iūppiter sē in taurum trānsfōrmat quod Eurōpa est timida. Eurōpa taurum spectat et taurus puellam portat. Nunc puella nōn est timida. Taurus fugitat et Eurōpam ad insulam Crētam portat. Deus et puella in insulā habitant.

Jupiter and Europa

Jupiter (Zeus) is a god and lives in Olympus. He watches the earth and sees the girl Europa. Europa is beautiful and Jupiter desires the girl. Jupiter transforms himself into a bull because Europa is timid. Europa looks at the bull and the bull carries the girl. Now the girl is not timid. The bull flees and brings Europa to the island Crete. The god and the girl live on the island.

Rōma

Rōma optima est. Viae Rōmānae dīrēctae sunt et aqua clara est. Hīc tunicae pulchrae sunt et arma splendida sunt. Volō hīc habitāre.

Rome

Rome is the best. The Roman roads are straight and the water is clear. Here there are beautiful tunics and the weapons are magnificent. I want to live here.

Fēlis et mūs

Fēlis ad silvam ambulat quod amīcum dēsīderat.
"Nonne hīc sunt amīcī," dīcit et in silvam ambulat.
Fēlis mūrem videt et mūs fēlem spectat. Deinde mūs fugat. Sed fēlis celer est
et mūrem cōnsequitur.
"Nōlī fugere!" fēlis clāmat. "Amīcum volō!"
"Fēlis et mūs amīcī nōn sunt!" clāmat mūs. "Quod fēlēs mūrēs edunt."
"Nōn mūrēs edō, quod dominus mihi cibum dat." dīcit fēlis.
"Nōn mūrēs edis?" rogat mūs.
"Ita est," dīcit fēlis. "Sumusne amīcī?"
"Ita est," dīcit mūs.

The Cat and the Mouse

A cat walks to the forest because she desires a friend.
"Surely there are friends here," she says and walks into the forest.
The cat sees a mouse and the mouse looks at the cat. Then the mouse flees.
But the cat is fast and chases the mouse.
"Don't run away!" the cat cries. "I want a friend!"
"A cat and mouse are not friends!" the mouse cries. "Because cats eat mice."
"I don't eat mice, because my master gives me food," says the cat.
"You don't eat mice?" asks the mouse.
"That's right," the cat says. "Are we friends?"
"Yes," says the mouse.

Pater Noster

Pater noster, quī es in caelīs,
sānctificētur nōmen tuum,
adveniat rēgnum tuum.
Fiat voluntās tua,
sicut in caelō, et in terrā.
Pānem nostrum quotīdiānum da nōbīs hodiē,
et dīmitte nōbīs dēbita nostra,
sicut et nōs dīmittimus dēbitōribus nostrīs.
Et nē nōs indūcās in tentātiōnem,
sed lība nōs a malō.

The Lord's Prayer

Our Father, who is in Heaven
may your name be glorified.
May your kingdom come;
may your will be done
on earth as it is in heaven.
Give us our daily bread today.
And forgive us our offenses,
as we forgive those who offend us.
And don't allow us to fall into temptation,
but liberate us from evil.

Sunt trēs parvī porcī et in mundum exīre volunt.
"Cavēte," dīcit māter et prīmus porcus parvus exit.
Domum aedificāre volat. Agricolam videt et dīcit, "Dā mihi strāmentum, quaesō." Et prīmus porcus parvus domum suam aedificat.

Deinde magnus lupus malus domum porcī videt. Lupus venit et dīcit, "Parve porce, parve porce, licetne mihi intrāre?"
"Nūllō modō!" prīmus porcus parvus clāmat.
Ergō magnus lupus malus inhālat et exhālat et domum dēlet. Deinde magnus lupus malus parvum porcum edit.

Secundus porcus parvus quoque domum aedificāre volat.
"Cavēte," dīcit māter et secundus porcus parvus exit. Silvam videt et lignum colligit. Deinde porcus parvus suam domum ē lignō aedificat.
Nunc magnus lupus malus venit et domum ligneam videt. Lupus dīcit, "Parve porce, parve porce licetne mihi intrāre?"
"Nūllō modō," secundus porcus parvus clāmat.
Ergō magnus lupus malus inhālat et exhālat et domum ligneam dēlet. Deinde magnus lupus malus parvum porcum edit.

Tertius porcus parvus quoque domum aedificāre volat sed callidus est.
"Cavēte," dīcit māter et tertius porcus parvus exit. Ad montem it et lapidēs colligit. Deinde porcus parvus suam domum ē lapide aedificat.
Nunc magnus lupus malus venit et domum lapideam videt. Lupus dīcit, "Parve porce, parve porce licetne mihi intrāre?"
"Nūllō modō," tertius porcus parvus clāmat.
Ergō magnus lupus malus inhālat et exhālat sed domum nōn dēlere potest. Lupus clāmat et inhālat et exhālat iterum et prīmus et secundus porcus ē lupō saliunt! Nunc lupus īrātus est et fugit.
Et trēs parvī porcī fēlīciter vivunt.

The Three Little Pigs

There are three little pigs and they want to go out in the world.
"Take care," says their mother and the first little pig leaves.
He wants to build a house. He sees a farmer and says, "Give me some straw,
please." And the first little pig builds his house.

Then the big bad wolf sees the pig's house. The wolf comes and says, "Little
pig, little pig, may I come in?"
"No way!" cries the first little pig. So the big bad wolf inhales and exhales and
destroys the house. Then the big bad wolf eats the little pig.

The second little pig also wants to build a house.
"Take care," says their mother and the second little pig leaves. He sees a
forest and collects wood. Then the little pig builds his house out of wood.
Now the big bad wolf comes and sees the house made of wood. The wolf
says, "Little pig, little pig, may I come in?"
"No way!" cries the second little pig. So the big bad wolf inhales and exhales
and destroys the house made of wood.
Then the big bad wolf eats the little pig.

The third little pig also wants to build a house, but is smart.
"Take care," says their mother and the third little pig leaves. He goes to the
mountain and collects stones. Then the little pig builds his house out of
stone.
Now the big bad wolf comes and sees the house made of stone. The wolf
says, "Little pig, little pig, may I come in?"
"No way!" cries the third little pig. So the big bad wolf inhales and exhales,
but can't destroy the house. The wolf screams and inhales and exhales again
and the first and second pig jump out of the wolf! Now the wolf is angry and
flees.
And the three little pigs live happily.

Maximus et Valentina

Hic est Maximus. Puer est. Hic puer discipulus est. Maximus est discipulus bonus.

Haec est Valentina. Puella est. Haec puella quoque discupula est. Valentina est discipula bona.

Hīc sunt Maximus et Valentina. Hic est Maximus. Maximus est frāter Valentinae. Haec est Valentina. Valentina est soror Maximī. ✳

Quis est haec? Haec fēmina est māter. Octavia est. Maximus est fīlius Octaviae. Valentina est fīlia Octaviae. Octavia māter Maximī et Valentinae est. Māter fīlium et fīliam amat.

Pater Maximī est Augustus. Augustus fortis est. Agricola est et in agrō lābōrat. Maximus patrī similis est. Valentina mātrī similis est. Octavia pulchra est. Ergō Valentina pulchra est. Maximus dīcit, "Soror mea pulchra est. Et māter mea quoque pulchra est."

Maximus et Valentina

This is Maximus. He is a boy. This boy is a student. Maximus is a good student.

This is Valentina. She is a girl. This girl is also a student. Valentina is a good student.

Here are Maximus and Valentina. This is Maximus. Maximus is Valentina's brother. This is Valentina. Valentina is Maximus' brother.

Who is this? This woman is a mother. She is Octavia. Maximus is Octavia's son. Valentina is Octavia's daughter. Octavia is Maximus' and Valentine's mother. The mother loves her son and daughter.

Maximus' father is Augustus. Augustus is strong. He is a farmer and works in the fields. Maximus is similar to his father. Valentina is similar to her mother. Octavia is beautiful. Therefore, Valentina is beautiful. Maximus says, "My sister is beautiful. And my mother is also beautiful."

Corvus et Vās

Ōlim corvus erat. Et hic corvus aquam bibere volēbat. Dum volābat, corvus vās vīdit.

Erat aqua in vāse. Sed satis aquae nōn erat et corvus nōn bibere poterat.

Nōn vās frangere poterat, quod nimis firmus erat. Postrēmō calculōs vīdit et problēma solvit.

Prīmō corvus calculōs ad vās portāvit. Deinde in vās posuit. Dēnique aqua ad summum pervēnit et corvus bibere poterat.

The Crow and the Vessel

Once upon a time, there was a crow. And this crow was thirsty. While it was flying, the crow saw a vase.

There was water in the vase. But there was not enough water and the crow could not drink.

It could not break the vase, because it was too strong. Finally, it saw pebbles and solved the problem.

First the crow carried the pebbles to the vase. Then it put them in the vase. Finally, the water reached the top and the crow could drink.

16

28, 36, 44, 46 83, 95, 99, 102   108

86, 87
88

Printed in Great Britain
by Amazon